THREE NOTELETS ON

SHAKESPEARE.

I. SHAKESPEARE IN GERMANY.

II. THE FOLK-LORE OF SHAKESPEARE.

III. WAS SHAKESPEARE EVER A SOLDIER?

BY WILLIAM J. THOMS, F.S.A.

LONDON:

JOHN RUSSELL SMITH,

SOHO-SQUARE.

1865.

TO

HER

WHO IN HERSELF REALIZES MANY OF SHAKESPEARE'S

TYPES OF WOMANLY EXCELLENCE,

AND TO WHOSE AFFECTIONATE COMPANIONSHIP

AND WISE COUNSELS

THE AUTHOR OWES ALL THE HAPPINESS HE HAS ENJOYED

FOR THE LAST SIX-AND-THIRTY YEARS,

THIS VOLUME

IS

DEDICATED.

PREFACE.

THE following Illustrations of the Life and Writings of Shakespeare are reprinted as they were originally published in 1840, 1847, and 1859, without addition and without alteration.

It would have been easy to have enlarged them, but for many reasons, I have not thought it expedient to do so. I have seen with pleasure that they have been found useful. With reference to several of the points which were first raised in them, subsequent writers have pursued the same line of inquiry* with excellent but as yet incomplete results.† I have thought that it might facilitate further investigation if they were gathered together out of the Journals in which they were first printed, and were published in a form in which they might be more easily accessible.

---

* In some cases with very little acknowledgment, and though my thunder may be as gentle as Bottom's roar, like Dennis, I claim my own.

† I am glad to learn that Mr. Albert Cohn, a gentleman who has enjoyed peculiar facilities for investigating the history of the early English Comedians in Germany, is about to publish a volume upon that interesting subject.

The desire to add my name in however humble a character to that band of brothers—like some other brothers occasionally not on the best terms with one another, but who all unite in the endeavour to illustrate the Life and Writings of our great Dramatist, has also operated in some slight degree to induce me to bring these papers together in the present volume. Many of Shakespeare's admirers look upon such comments with distaste, and liken the writers to the thoughtless and giddy who scratch their names on every spot they visit, from a bench in Greenwich Park to the Pyramids of Egypt.

But all names are not so inscribed from foolish or unworthy motives. On the monument of Isaac Casaubon, in Poets' Corner, may be seen the well-known monogram of good old Isaac Walton, graven, there can be no doubt, by his own hand, in love and admiration of that departed worthy.

In that same spirit,

> " On the vast monument of Shakespeare's fame
> With reverent hand, I write my humble name."

WILLIAM J. THOMS.

40, St. George's Square,
16th Nov. 1864.

I.

SHAKESPEARE IN GERMANY.

(1840.)

THE following Letter was written at the request of the kind friend to whom it was addressed, for the purpose of being communicated to the Society of Antiquaries on the 21st May, 1840, when the late Prince Consort attended and signed the List of Fellows. But His Royal Highness having promised to attend the Royal Society after leaving the Antiquaries, there was not time for the reading of any papers, and this communication was consequently made to the Society on the following Thursday.

Mr. Theodore Hooke, who was present at the reading, having expressed a wish to publish it in the "New Monthly Magazine," which was then under his editorship, it was printed in the July 1840 Number of that Journal.

ON THE

CONNECTION BETWEEN THE EARLY ENGLISH
AND EARLY GERMAN DRAMA,
AND ON THE PROBABLE ORIGIN OF
SHAKESPEARE'S "TEMPEST."

In a Letter to Thomas Amyot, Esq., F.R.S., Treas. S. A.

MY DEAR SIR,

REASONS for addressing the present letter to you, are as plenty as blackberries; and I need no compulsion, nor is it necessary that I should be at the strappado or all the racks in the world, to give you two of them. The first is, that you take an interest, and are well versed in all matters connected with Shakespeare and his contemporaries, and have done good services to Shakespearian literature ; and the second, because it affords me an opportunity of acknowledging and thanking you for many acts of kindness, not the least of them being your introduction of me to that Prospero, whose library was dukedom large enough, but whose cell is now untenanted, whose staff is broken, and with its great master now

> "Buried certain fathoms in the earth "—

I mean of course our much regretted friend, the late

Mr. Douce, who would, I am sure, had he been living, have read with some interest the observations to which I now beg to call your attention.

It is many years since I first " made a prief in my note-book," that at the close of the sixteenth and commencement of the seventeenth century, Germany was visited by a company of English players; but never, until very recently, have I had an opportunity of referring to the authority for this statement, and ascertaining the more minute particulars which are there recorded, relative to this curious and, hitherto, unnoticed fact in the history of the early English drama.

That the dramatists of England exercised a great and beneficial influence in the direction which they gave to the genius of their German brethren, has never been questioned. The German critics have for the most part agreed upon this point, which has been more especially insisted upon by Tieck, distinguished among his countrymen, not only as a poet, a novelist, and a critic, but also for his deeper reverence and profounder knowledge of our immortal bard—to the study of whose writings, and those of his contemporaries, many years of his life have been almost exclusively devoted. He it was, moreover, who first showed how actively and immediately this influence was employed, by proving that about the year 1600, many of the productions of the English dramatists were translated into German, and performed before the German public by a company of comedians, who were known at that time as the English company.

This singular fact was first announced by Tieck in the year 1817, when he commenced the publication of his " German Theatre," a work which was intended

to furnish his countrymen with a selection of the most
remarkable productions of the German stage, which,
from being scattered throughout a number of volumes,
many of them of the greatest rarity, were for the most
part inaccessible to the general reader. In short,
Tieck intended to do for the German drama what
Dodsley had so successfully accomplished for the
English. But though he proposed to extend his collection to six volumes only, he met with so little
encouragement, that no more than the first and second
ever appeared. Each volume has a preface illustrative
of the works it contains, with an account of their
authors, and the state of the stage when they wrote—
the plays themselves being arranged chronologically.
In the first volume there are two of the Shrovetide
plays by Hans Rosenplut, six pieces by Hans Sachs,
five by Jacob Ayrer, and one from the German collection of English plays, to which I shall presently have
occasion to direct your attention. It is in his remarks
upon the life and writings of Ayrer, that Tieck mentions the circumstance to which I have already alluded.

Jacob Ayrer, the successor of Hans Sachs as a
writer for the German stage, was a proctor and notary at Nuremberg, where he lived probably till about
1618, in which year, and as it appears shortly after
his death, the goodly folio which contains his "Opus
Dramaticum," was first published in that city. Nothing further indeed is known of him, nor even the
date of his birth, nor the period during which he
wrote his numerous dramas. Koch says he composed
his several works between 1570 and 1589, but adduces
no evidence in support of this statement. Gottsched
mentions his German version of Frischlin's "Julius

Redivivus," as being published at Worms in 1585; but from internal evidence it is obvious that it was written in 1610; whilst, from a passage in his Whitsun play of " The Process against the Tyranny of Queen Podagra," it is clear that that piece was written in 1602.

Tieck, who was of opinion that, with the exception perhaps of his Whitsun plays, few of Ayrer's pieces were written before 1610, describes them as consisting partly of imitations of English models, and partly of original pieces written in the style of his prototype Hans Sachs, with the addition of a professed jester or merry-maker, whom he styles sometimes Jahn Posset, sometimes the English fool, occasionally also Jahn Clahm, from which it may be inferred, that when he drew the character, he had the clown of the old English drama before his eyes.

It is when showing the means by which Ayrer acquired a knowledge of the models from which he is supposed to have copied, that Tieck brings forward the fact, that, about the year 1600, a company of comedians called the English Company traversed Germany, performing German translations of English plays at all the principal courts and chief cities of the empire.

" Such," said Tieck, " was the popularity which the stage enjoyed in London, and such was its reputation on the continent, that troops of players occasionally proceeded to the Netherlands, for the purpose of exhibiting their performances; and we can trace in Germany about the year 1600 (probably some years earlier), the existence of a company of comedians who, under the title of the English Company, travelled the country round, for the purpose of giving the German public some idea, however imperfect, of the height which poetry and the dramatic art had attained in England." He adds, that he had himself ascertained the dates of the years in which these comedians performed before the court of Dresden, but had unfortunately mislaid the notes he had made of them.

Tieck does not decide who these actors really were; whether they were natives of England; or young Germans connected with the Hanse Company, then established in London; or persons who had travelled from Germany to England on a theatrical speculation, for the purpose of securing a stock of new dramas; but his description of the volume of German translations of English plays, published in Germany in 1620, which he supposes to have emanated from them, would seem to favour the supposition that they were, as their name implies, a company of English players. The same inference may be drawn from one clear instance which Tieck gives of English actors being found in Germany. He is speaking of the marks of distinction with which professed players were then received in that country, and after stating that the magistrates of the different cities were in the habit of going out to meet them on their approach, he adds that Lassenius, one of the earliest actors whose name is preserved, and who, as he was playing about the year 1600, might possibly have belonged to this very troop, became afterwards a doctor of theology; and another Hans von Stockfisch (probably an assumed theatrical name), received a salary of two hundred dollars, and other allowances, from John Sigmund of Brandenburg, for whom he procured a company of comedians *from England* and the Netherlands about the year 1614.

Tieck, who regards the English company of come-

dians as having exercised an extraordinary influence
on the German drama, by the direction which they
gave to the theatrical compositions of Jacob Ayrer,
describes very fully the extremely interesting volume
which he supposes to have emanated from them.   It
was first printed in 1620, and its quaint, old-fashioned
title, may be thus translated: "English Comedies
and Tragedies; that is, right pleasant, noble and
select, spiritual and worldly Comedies and Tragedies,
with the humours of Pickle Herring—which on account of their pleasant invention, merry conceits, and
true histories, have been acted and performed by the
Englishmen in Germany, at the royal, electoral, and
princely courts, and in all the great free cities of the
empire, but have never before been printed.   Now
published and set forth for the gratification and delight of all lovers of comedy and tragedy, &c. &c."

   To this volume a second and a third were subsequently added; neither of them, however, contains
any thing of importance.   But the original collection,
which is of exceeding rarity, although a second edition
appeared in 1630, contains, in addition to a number
of interludes, merriments, or jigs, no less than eight
old English dramatic pieces, translated into the very
commonest German prose, printed very incorrectly,
and in a language which seems to have been written
down from the recitation of unskilful actors, being
filled with uncouth phrases and words misapplied—
the construction of the sentences any thing but German, and the whole abounding with coarse equivoques
and obscene allusions.   The first of these is the
" History of Esther and Haman," which Tieck speaks
of as having been played in London in 1594, and even
earlier, and which we learn from Mr. Collier's ad-

mirable Annals of the Stage, was printed by William Pickering, in 1561. Tieck describes this piece, though a mere sketch, as being clearly the work of a theatrical poet who understood stage effect, so that the arrangement and connection of the scenes betray quite a different spirit from the historical plays of Hans Sachs, or those which Ayrer composed when not imitating a foreign model. The comic character in it, who is called Hans Knapcase, has the same struggles for mastery with his wife as the Jahn Posset of Ayrer's Whitsun play, and Edward III., but with some additional jests. Hans is the carpenter who builds the gallows for Haman, who, however, hangs himself, so that Hans is unnecessarily dragged into the scene.

The second is the " Prodigal Son," which Tieck describes as being more skilfully and cleverly composed.

This is followed by the " History of Fortunatus," which Tieck has reprinted in the second volume of his collection, and respecting which he remarks that it is interesting to observe how skilfully the author has treated the subject, which is one by no means well adapted to the stage. A play with the title of " Fortunatus" had been performed in London, in 1595, or earlier. It was remodelled in 1600 by Decker, who, from the subject being so well known, entitled his work " The Old Fortunatus." This remodelled version by Decker, which, whatever may now be thought of it, laid the foundation of the celebrity which he afterwards enjoyed, was not the one used by the English company in Germany; and from this circumstance Tieck concludes, and apparently with great reason, that they had left London some time before the year 1600.

The fourth piece, which appears to be one of the oldest, is " a triumphant comedy," entitled, "Of a Son of the King of England, and a Daughter of the King of Scotland." The plot is very simple, and turns upon the circumstance of the English Prince, during a war with England and Scotland, falling in love with the daughter of his enemy, and procuring a truce in order that he may visit his beloved in the disguise of a jester. The prince, who is called *Serule*, being the comic character of the piece, there is no clown introduced into it.

The fifth play, which bears the fewest traces of its English origin, is called " Sidonea and Theagenea," and consists of a mere love story, during the progress of which the peasant *Cnemon* and his sweetheart are by no means sparing of coarse jests.

The sixth of these dramas is one of the most remarkable, from the very bold manner in which it combines old English history and allegory. It abounds in satire, which is very spirited, even in the wretched translation, and is the same piece which was printed in London in 1603, under the title of " Nobody and Somebody; with the true chronicle History of Elydure, who was fortunately three times crowned King of England."

This is followed by the tragedy of " Julio and Hypolita," which is almost the same as Shakespeare's " Two Gentlemen of Verona," except that in the German piece, at the wedding, the deceived friend stabs the false one, who has certainly carried on his intrigue very clumsily—the bride murders herself, and her lover follows her example. The clown of the play is called *Grobianus Pickleherring*. Tieck tells us that the piece is only very roughly and briefly given, much

of it appearing to be omitted, as is indeed obviously
the case with most of the others in this collection;
yet, as it is in all probability a translation of an earlier
English play than Shakespeare's, it is much to be wished
that Tieck had reprinted it, that some idea might have
been formed of the materials out of which Shakespeare
fashioned what his last editor pronounces "his first
complete comedy:" for, if the supposition be correct
that an earlier English play existed on the same subject as the "Two Gentlemen of Verona," it will
be but reasonable to conclude that it was to such play,
and not to the "Diana" of George Montemayor, that
Shakespeare was indebted for his plot.

The eighth and last of these plays is " Titus Andronicus." Tieck, who has reprinted it in his fifth
volume, says, " This most horrible tragedy was an
especial favourite with the London public, before
whom, from the year 1593 it was frequently performed. Shakespeare re-wrote it in 1600, and gave it
the form which it now assumes in the collection of
his works. None but the uncritical English editors
could, in the face of contemporaries, the published
impression of it, and all signs of authenticity, pronounce it on the score of its inferiority alone not to
be genuine; and since Shakespeare re-wrote it, withdrew it from another theatre, and represented it upon
his own, the probability is that the earlier 'Andronicus' was written by him. The German translation
is only a version of the 'Andronicus' in its first form,
and that, moreover, an abbreviated one; for the mur-
dered sons of *Titus* do not appear in it or contribute
to the action of the piece, while the assumed madness
of *Titus*, which suggests to the empress the idea of
disguising herself as *Revenge*, is passed over in silence,

by which means the keeping of the latter part of the
poem is destroyed. On the other hand, its extra-
vagant horrors are every where exaggerated, yet it is
easy to discover, scattered here and there throughout
the piece, passages which are all but literally translated from the poet's verses; and this old piece must
therefore be considered as of the highest value, since
it affords us a tolerably. clear view of this youthful
work of Shakespeare, and we are enabled by means of
this fragment to compare it with his later version of
it."

Tieck then proceeds to justify himself in the eyes
of his German readers for reprinting the " Titus
Andronicus," and " Fortunatus ; " " which," he says,
" considering the wretched language in which they
are written, are only deserving their attention partly
as literary curiosities and partly as strangers, which
having been received with welcome on their arrival
in the country, have now come to be looked upon as
originally belonging to it ; " and he numbers among
subjects of foreign growth now naturalized in Germany, " Faustus "—for he supposes the " Faustus "
of Marlowe, and some very remarkable pieces of which
traces are discoverable in the writings of Ayrer, to
have been introduced at the same time into that country by the English comedians.

Before I conclude this part of my subject, in which
I hope I have contributed some fresh materials, however trifling they may be considered, towards the literary history of the drama, and of two of Shakespeare's
compositions, let me add, that our friend, the Rev.
Joseph Hunter, has for some time possessed evidence
of early English players visiting the continent; the
knowledge of which he arrived at while pursuing those

researches to which we are indebted for his interesting
"Dissertation on the Tempest."

And now, having shown you how Jacob Ayrer was
enabled, by means of these wanderers, to acquire a
knowledge of the various dramas performing on the
English stage towards the close of the sixteenth century, I next beg to call your attention to a few of the
productions of this worthy notary of Nuremberg,
among which we shall find translations of two other
early English dramas, which, if I am right in my belief, furnished Shakespeare with the groundwork of
two of the most striking of his matchless compositions.

Ayrer appears to have been a very voluminous
writer, being the author of no less than thirty dramas,
besides six-and-thirty Whitsun plays, which latter,
although they appear to have been printed as early as
1610, were not given to the public until they appeared
in the complete collection of his works, published in
1618. Among these Whitsun plays, to which Tieck
considers the jigs of the old English theatre as bearing
the closest possible resemblance, are several which he
pronounces to be unquestionably derived from English sources; one of the chief reasons which have led
him to this conclusion being the fact of the clown of
these pieces being represented with a fife or tabor—
a constant practice on the English stage, but of which
no traces are to be found in the national fools of the
German, Spanish, Italian, and French theatres. And,
therefore, although one of the Whitsun plays " Der
Uberwundene Trummelschläger" (the Vanquished
Drummer) is thoroughly Germanised, he does not
hesitate to pronounce it an English farce, and suggests whether the old proverbial allusion to " Jack
Drum's entertainment," may not have originated from

some such merriment—the old play, printed in 1616, under that title (of which the German piece is not, as might be supposed, a translation), affording no illustration of the source from which the saying is derived.

Again, of the thirty dramas written by Ayrer—though five are founded on events recorded in the "History of Rome"—still in some of these the English clown plays his part, while, with the exception of three which are taken from the "Heldenbuch," the tragedy of "Theseus," and four long pieces on the subject of "Valentine and Orson," which may be original (though these last exhibit traces of old English books), the majority of his compositions contain decided proofs of their English origin, and of their author's acquaintance with the English stage. His "History of the Emperor Mahomet, and the Siege of Constantinople," might have been derived from the well-known accounts of the taking of that city; but it is far from improbable that he borrowed it from the drama which George Peele wrote upon that subject, and the popularity of which is supposed to be established by Pistol's exclamation, "Have we not Hiren here?" Again, his "Getreue Ramo" and "Edward III." are supposed to be taken from English plays founded on popular romances; while his play, "Von zween fürstlichen Räthen die beide um ein Weib buhlten" (Of the two prince's councillors who courted one woman), is decidedly copied from an English original; and his "Alt Buhler" (old lover) is a somewhat amplified version of the farce or jig, "Die schöne Maria," one of the five pieces of that description printed in the collection of the English comedians.

But leaving these general assertions, and coming to plain facts, we find that his comedy of the "King

of Cyprus and Queen of France," is nearly identical,
scene for scene, with the " Dumb Knight " of Lewis
Machin and Gervase Markham, printed in 1608, and
reprinted in Dodsley's old plays, vol. iv., Collier's
edition. While his play of "Belimperia and Horatio,"
which Tieck has reprinted in the first volume of his
collection, is nothing more than a German version of
" The Spanish Tragedy, or Hieronymo is Mad again,"
which it follows scene for scene, and name for name,
with this exception, that out of anxious consideration
for the Emperor, Ayrer has changed the locality from
Spain to Greece, and entitled the King Amurath, and
the Marshal Malignus, instead of Hieronymo. Tieck,
who gives it as his opinion that the original old play
of " The Spanish Tragedy " laid the foundation of the
tragic drama of England, speaks of it as having been
played in London as early as 1570, (but produces no
evidence in support of this statement, which is possibly a misprint for 1590), being afterwards re-written
and enlarged by Kyd in 1593 and 1597 ; and states
that it is from this old play in its earlier form, that
Ayrer derived his drama. That the latter part of this
statement is correct, there can, I think, be little doubt.

But the next of Ayrer's pieces which Tieck has
reprinted, possesses still greater attraction for the
English reader, more especially if Tieck be correct
in his supposition (and there seems no reason to doubt
that he is so) that it is an adaptation from the English.
It is entitled " Phœnizia," and like Shakespeare's
" Much Ado about Nothing," is founded on Bandello's
well-known novel, entitled " Fenicia."   In fact, Tieck
looks upon Ayrer's play as being a German version
of the earlier English drama, on which Shakespeare
founded his admirable comedy ; and Tieck is, I have

no doubt, perfectly right in this supposition. One instance will, I think, prove that Shakespeare did not derive his plot directly from Bandello. In the novel, Timbreo (the *Claudio* of the play), witnesses the hired servant of Girondo in the dress of a gentleman, ascending a ladder to the chamber of Fenicia; but in Shakespeare's play this incident is altered, and that too for the worse. " Shakespeare," says Skottowe, " again deviates from the novel when he desires to excite jealousy in *Claudio,* who witnesses an amorous conversation between *Borachio* and the waiting-woman of *Hero,* disguised in the clothes of her mistress. *Borachio* addresses *Margaret* throughout by the name of *Hero.* Probability is violated in this case; for as *Claudio* is supposed to be near enough to hear distinctly the dialogue contrived for his deception, he must have been stupid beyond all calculation not to have discovered that the pretended lady, neither in voice nor person, resembled *Hero.*"

But if Tieck be correct in supposing that Shakespeare derived his plot from the earlier English play from which Ayrer has copied his " Phœnicia," it is not Shakespeare, but his prototype, who is in this instance in fault; for in the German version we find *Timbreo* not only witnesses the ascent of *Gerwalt* to *Phœnicia's* chamber; but, like Shakespeare's *Claudio,* he overhears an amorous conversation between *Gerwalt* and *Jahn* the clown of the piece, and the servant of *Gerando* disguised as *Phœnicia*—and this fact alone furnishes a strong presumption, that Shakespeare was indebted not to Bandello, but to some earlier dramatist for the plot of this comedy. A careful perusal of the old German play has indeed satisfied my mind that it is derived from an earlier English play; and should some unlooked-for piece of good fortune ever unearth it, I have no doubt that, like Ayrer's drama, it will be found to commence with a mythological introduction in which Venus and Cupid play conspicuous parts, but which Shakespeare altogether rejected, although it had not altogether faded from his memory when he penned Benedict's witticisms upon the subject of the "Blind God."

But important as *I* consider this fact to be, as illustrative of the sources to which Shakespeare was indebted for his plots, you will probably agree with me in thinking the next as still more so. "The origin of the plot of the ' Tempest ' is for the present a Shakespearian mystery," are the words of our friend Mr. Hunter, in his learned and interesting dissertation upon that play. That mystery, however, I consider as solved—Tieck appears to entertain no doubt upon the subject—and I hope to bring the matter before you in such a manner, as will satisfy you of the correctness of Tieck's views in this respect. But to the point—Shakespeare unquestionably derived his idea of the "Tempest" from an earlier drama, now not known to exist, but of which a German version is preserved in Ayrer's play entitled "Die Schöne Sidea" (the beautiful Sidea); and the proof of this fact is to be found in the points of resemblance between the two plays, which are far too striking and peculiar to be the result of accident.

It is true that the scene in which Ayrer's play is laid, and the names of the personages differ from those of the "Tempest;" but the main incidents of the two plays are all but identically the same. For instance, in the German drama, *Prince Ludolph* and *Prince Leudegast* supply the places of *Prospero* and

c

Alonzo.   Ludolph, like *Prospero*, is a magician, and like him has an only daughter *Sidea*—the Miranda of the " Tempest"—and an attendant spirit *Runcifal*, who, though not strictly resembling either *Ariel* or *Caliban*, may well be considered as the primary type which suggested to the nimble fancy of our great dramatist, those strongly yet admirably contrasted beings. Shortly after the commencement of the play, *Ludolph* having been vanquished by his rival, and with his daughter *Sidea* driven into a forest, rebukes her for complaining of their change of fortune, and then summons his spirit *Runcifal* to learn from him their future destiny, and prospects of revenge. *Runcifal*, who is, like *Ariel*, somewhat " moody," announces to *Ludolph* that the son of his enemy will shortly become his prisoner.   After a comic episode, most probably introduced by the German, we see *Prince Leudegast*, with his son *Engelbrecht*—the Ferdinand of the " Tempest"—and the councillors, hunting in the same forest; when *Engelbrecht* and his companion *Famulus*, having separated from their associates, are suddenly encountered by *Ludolph* and his daughter. He commands them to yield themselves prisoners— they refuse, and try to draw their swords, when, as *Prospero* tells *Ferdinand*,

> " I can here disarm thee with this stick,
> And make thy weapon drop,"

so *Ludolph*, with his wand, keeps their swords in their scabbards, paralyzes *Engelbrecht*, and makes him confess his

> " —Nerves are in their infancy again,
> And have no vigour in them,"

and when he has done so gives him over as a slave to *Sidea, to carry logs for her.*

The resemblance between this scene and the parallel scene in the " Tempest," is rendered still more striking in a late part of the play, when *Sidea*, moved by pity for the labours of *Engelbrecht*, in *carrying logs*, declares to him,

"I am your wife, if you will marry me,"

an event which, in the end, is happily brought about and leads to the reconciliation of their parents, the rival princes.

And now, my dear sir, when you consider these several particulars, and that Tieck, who is himself an eminent German critic, pronounces the work of his countryman to be most decidedly an imitation of an earlier English play—although we no longer possess that play—I say, when you consider all these things, can you refuse your assent to the conclusion to which Tieck arrived long since, that it is *more than probable* that Ayrer's " Sidea," and Shakespeare's " Tempest," "alike, but oh, how different!" were both derived from one common source, and that an earlier English drama.

Before I conclude this communication, which has grown under my pen to an extent far beyond what I originally intended, I would fain avail myself of the opportunity it affords me of calling the attention of the Shakespearian commentators to two or three points connected with the " Tempest," which appear to me deserving of more attention than they have yet received.

Mr. Hunter has already noticed how much that is Hebraistic this play contains; and assuredly if we examine the peculiarities by which the magic of *Prospero* is characterized, we see at once from its oriental colouring, that he must have "learned the art which none may name," among the adepts of the east, most probably among the descendants of Solomon, whose dominion over the world of spirits formed, according to legendary tale, the source of his wisdom.

Now when we remember this, and also that one of the most remarkable events in the history of Lampedusa is its being the scene where the fleet of Charles the Fifth was shipwrecked, and bear in mind how an event of this importance must have directed attention to the island during the sixteenth century; and learn, moreover, that there exists among the Jews a tradition that the very tempest that dispersed it, and thereby rendered the island remarkable, was raised by the magical skill of an Algerine Jew, who "put the wild waters in a roar," one cannot help suspecting that Shakespeare had heard the story, and engrafted upon the old play, to which he was indebted for the hints of his plot, all the learning which he possessed connected with oriental magic and Jewish tradition.

The whole of the supernatural machinery of the play is, indeed, deeply tinged with Jewish superstition. I need not stop to show you how completely *Prospero* answers to the generally-received idea of a cabalistic philosopher, nor detain you with speculations on the resemblance which *Caliban* bears to the *fish-idol* of Ashdod, the Dagon of the Philistines, for these points have been already ably illustrated by Mr. Hunter; but I must call your attention to the connection which exist between *Ariel* and the Jewish spirits שׁדים (Schedim). Mr. Hunter speaks of Shakespeare as either "inventing a name not before in the spiritual vocabulary, or adopting one from the undiscovered writer whom he follows;" and says further, "that in the *dramatis personæ, Ariel* is described as 'an airy spirit,' and the resemblance in the sound of this word to this description was, perhaps, the sole circumstance which determined Shakespeare to the choice, if it were a choice and not an invention." Mr. Hunter also refers to that part of the Prophet Isaiah, in which *Ariel*, the Lion of God,* is used as a personation of Jerusalem—adding, " that some of the attributes and feats of *Ariel* may seem to have been suggested by what he read in that prophet." That Shakespeare learned the name of *Ariel* from his Bible, and selected it from the resemblance its sound bore to the character of his quaint spirit, and that some of the feats and attributes of that spirit were suggested by the words of Isaiah, is extremely probable; but, at the same time, it is important to know, as confirmatory of the Hebraistic character of this glorious play, that *Ariel* not only answers to the description of the Jewish spirits, Schedim,† but that *Ariel* (אריאל)‡ is the name of one of the

---

* The learning of the commentators on the use of the name *Ariel*, in the text, is well condensed in an introductory paragraph to an admirable sermon preached by Melvill, on 5th November, 1837.

† Sale, in his " Introduction to the Koran," I. 96 (ed. 1801), says, " The Mahommedan notions concerning these genii, agree almost exactly with what the Jews write of a sort of demons called Schedim, whom some fancy to have been begotten by two angels, named Aza and Azaël, on Naamah the daughter of Lamech, before the flood. However, the Schedim, they tell us, agree in three things with the ministering angels; for that, like them, *they have wings, and fly from one end of the world to the other, and have some knowledge of futurity;* and in three things they agree with men like whom they eat and drink, are propagated and die. They also say that some of them believe in the law of Moses and are consequently good, and that others of them are infidels and reprobates."

‡ So it is stated in the book " Berith Menûcha," fol. 37, col. 1.,

seven princes of angels or spirits who preside over
waters under Micael, the arch-prince, and that therefore *Prospero* might well inquire of him,

——" Hast thou, spirit,
Performed to points the Tempest that I bade thee ? "

I have now, my dear sir, laid before you my small
store of that knowledge illustrative of Shakespeare, of
which Johnson said " every man has some, and none
much," and I have done so, trusting to your kindness
as much as to its own merits, to give it welcome.

Believe me,

My dear sir,

Your obliged and very faithful servant,

WILLIAM J. THOMS.

---

where we learn also that another spirit *Hariel,* or, as it is written
in other copies, *Ariel,* has dominion over cattle. Heywood, on
the other hand, in his " Hierarchie of the Blessed Angels" (lib.
iv. p. 216-217), ascribes to Ariel supremacy on the earth,

" Others there be, that do not doubt to say,
That the foure Elements are forced t'obey,
Foure severall Angels ; *Seraph* reigns o'er Fire ;
Cherub the Aire ; and *Tharsis* doth aspire
Over the water ; and the Earth's great Lord
Ariel. The Hebrew Rabbins thus accord."

And explaining the origin of these names, adds,

" For instance, *Seraph,* if we but retyre
To the word's force, importeth nought save fire :
Cherub, aire : *Tharsus,* water : *Ariel,* earth."

And in his notes upon this book, Heywood furnishes us with
the following illustration of the belief upon which the character
and agency of *Ariel* in the "Tempest" is founded—" Saint
Augustine in his booke ' De Cognitione Veræ Vitæ " is per-
suaded that Spirits by God's permission can raise Stormes and
Tempests, and command raine, hail, snow, thunder, and light-
ning, at their pleasures."

II.

THE FOLK-LORE OF SHAKESPEARE.

(1847.)

The following Papers appeared in the "Athenæum" during the year 1847. The circumstances under which they were written are stated in the Introduction prefixed to them. The present writer may perhaps be permitted here to put upon record that the term "Folk-Lore," which was so universally accepted as in less than a twelvemonth to have arrived at the dignity of a household word, was first introduced by him, under the pseudonym of Ambrose Merton, in his communication to the "Athenæum" of the 22nd August, 1846.

THE FOLK-LORE OF SHAKESPEARE.

THOSE readers of the "Athenæum" who take an interest in our English "Folk-Lore" will, doubtless, remember that the articles so entitled which have from time to time appeared in these columns, were evoked by an intimation that "communications on such subjects from earnest and well-informed correspondents" would be welcome. They may remember, too, that such intimation was given at the suggestion of a correspondent signing himself "Ambrose Merton," who, in soliciting the aid of the "Athenæum" for preserving the infinite number of minute facts illustrative of this branch of antiquarian learning scattered over the memories of its many readers, confessed to a personal interest in the success of his appeal—on the ground of his having long contemplated a work in connection with English Folk-Lore.

That correspondent was the present writer; and the work to which he referred was one in which he proposed to make the writings of Shakespeare and that Folk-Lore which the poet loved, mutually illustrative of each other. The papers under the above special heading which may from time to time appear in our columns, are fragments of that attempt to throw a light over the writings of the Poet of the People from the side of our popular literature, customs, and superstitions.

I. SHAKESPEARE'S FAIRY LORE.

" Then since no muse hath been so bold,
    Or of the later, or the old,
    Those elvish secrets to unfold
        Which lie from others reading;
    My active muse to light shall bring
    The court of that proud fairy king,
    And tell there of the revelling :
        Jove prosper my proceeding ! "

                                        DRAYTON's *Nymphidia.*

HOSE, alone, who have made Popular Antiquities, and more especially Popular Mythology, an object of study can thoroughly appreciate the difficulty of forming anything approaching to a proper classification of the facts which exist upon those subjects. Neither the " Popular Antiquities " of Brande, nor that far more important work the " German Mythology " of James Grimm, furnishes any arrangement which could be followed with advantage on the present occasion.

A mere glance at the writings of Shakespeare must convince us that the fairy mythology of England— of which, as has been elsewhere observed, " he was the best and most beautiful expositor "—was that branch of our Folk-Lore which he most ardently admired and most successfully employed ; and it seems to be only a fitting homage to his judgment that our earliest attention should be devoted to illustrate the history of the

" Elves of hills, brooks, standing lakes, and groves;
 And ye, that on the sands with printless foot
 Do chase the ebbing Neptune, and do fly him
 When he comes back; you demy-puppets, that
 By moonshine do the green-sour ringlets make
 Whereof the ewe not bites; and you whose pastime
 Is to make midnight mushrooms."

In the above beautiful invocation (in which Warburton's classical prejudices could only see an imitation
of that of Medea—

" Auræque, et venti, montesque, amnesque, lacusque,
 Diique omnes nemorum, diique omnes noctis, adeste "—

although, as Boswell justly remarks, Ovid has not
supplied anything resembling the exquisite fairy
imagery with which Shakespeare has enriched his
speech) the various elements that go to form the fairy
mythology of Shakespeare are intimately blended.
And so intimate, indeed, is this union,—so closely
have the centuries which have gone to their formation
interwoven the Celtic with the Teutonic, and these
two with the modifications consequent upon the introduction of Christianity—that it is no longer possible
to say with certainty the points at which the one
ceases and the other has supplanted it.

For however earnestly the reader may join with
Falstaff in exclaiming, " Heaven defend me from a
Welsh fairy, lest he transform me to a piece of
cheese!"—however imperfect may be our records of
Welsh or Ancient British fairy lore—it is not the less
certain that the Fairies of Shakespeare, and of many
of our fireside stories, are indebted for several of the
characteristics with which they are invested, both
in the works of our poets and in the stories of our
old crones, to their Celtic descent. " The fairies of

Europe," says a learned German,* who has obviously
been led to investigate their history from its connection with that of the Celtic races, "belong originally
to the Celts, from whom, with their accompanying
legends, they first passed over to the Germans." He
is very possibly right; for he is speaking of such
fairies as those to whom Milton alludes, as

> " Faery damsels met in forests wide
> By Knights of Logres, or of Lyones,
> Lancelot, or Pelleas, or Pellenore,"—

who had originally nothing in common with those
elves and dwarfs to whom the name is now so universally—but, with deference be it spoken, so improperly
—applied. Mr. Keightley—the introductory chapter
of whose interesting " Fairy Mythology " is devoted
to an investigation into the origin of the word Fairy
—is of opinion that "after the appearance of the
'Faerie Queene' all distinctions were confounded;
the names and attributes of the real Fays or Fairies
of romance were completely transferred to the little
beings who, according to the popular belief, made
'the green-sour ringlets whereof the ewe not bites.'
The change thus operated by the poets established
itself firmly among the people:—a strong proof, if
this idea be correct, of the power of the poetry of a
nation in altering the phraseology of even the lowest
classes of its society. Shakespeare must be regarded
as a principal agent in this revolution."

Without being prepared, with Mr. Keightley, to
ascribe this confusion of the Celtic Fairy with the
Teutonic Elf to the influence of Spenser's splendid

---

* Schreiber—" Die Feen in Europa." See also his Essay,
entitled " Feen und Hexen."

Allegory *——or, indeed, to admit that such confusion
did not exist at a far earlier period, (for it is obvious
that when Chaucer speaks of

" The Elf-quene with her joly compagnie,"

he invests the Celtic fairy with a name which does
not properly belong to her)—we are quite ready to
concede that after the two classes had become so
closely identified by Shakespeare, after he had once
joined   •

" Elves and Fairies in a ring,"

it was not to be expected that when

" Their midnight revels by a forest side,
Or fountain, some belated peasant sees,
Or dreams he sees,"

he should readily mark the difference between the
Fairies who are properly the descendants of the
Druidesses of old—and the Elves, who boast their
origin from, and their connection with, the Duergar
of the North.

A confusion of names has obviously contributed to
this confusion of attributes. " The very name Fairy,"
says Schreiber, " betrays its Celtic origin "—" and
points to the Romance *Fada*, the Italian *Fata*, and
Spanish *Hada*."† Grimm, on the other hand, treating
of the relationship between *Parca* and *Fatum*, speaks

---

* Though this would seem to be supported by the closing
note of Dr. Johnson on the " Midsummer Night's Dream : "
" Fairies in his [Shakespeare's] time were much in fashion ;
:ommon tradition had made them familiar, and Spenser's poem
uad made them great." -

† See further, on the connection of the more modern Fairies
with the Druidical system on the one hand and the Classical
Mythology on the other, Alfred Maury, " Les Fées du Moyen-
Age."

of the impersonation of this latter word in the Romance tongue after the *Parcæ* had disappeared from
the imagination of the people; but is doubtful as to
whether such impersonation was called forth by the
influence of the female divinities of the Celtic mythology or of those of the German Norns. Of the Fairies
of romance there exist a number of traditions corresponding to those which exist in the Folk-Lore of
Germany. Folquet de Puar sings—

> " Aissim *fadero tres serors*
> En aquella ora qu ieu sui natz
> Que totz temps fos enamoratz ; "

Guilhaume de Poitou—

> " Aissi fuy de nueitz *fadatz* sobr' un puegau ; "

and Marcabrus—

> " *Gentil fada*
> Vos adastret, quan fos nada,
> Duna beutat esmerada. "

In the remarkable collection of Neapolitan tales,
by Giambattista Basile, entitled, " Il Pentamerone,"[*]
we have frequent mention of *certe Fate*; one story
especially, named " Le Tre Fate,"—and one entitled
" Le Sette Cotenelle," which is nearly identical with
" Die Drei Spinnerinnen " of Grimm and of the various
cognate legends of the North. Cervantes, too, in his
" Don Quixote," mentions " los siete Castillos de las
siete Fadas."[†] The Fairies, again, to whom Brun

---

[*] It is rather a remarkable circumstance, that among the
curious notes which Felix Liebrecht, the recent editor of this
work, has collected, he has not devoted any to the illustration
of the " Fate," and the popular notions of the Neapolitans with
regard to them.

[†] Grimm, " Deutsche Mythologie," s. 383.

de la Montagne is presented at the fountain in the Forest of the Brocheliande, as we learn from the romance so entitled, (fragments of which have been printed by M. Le Roux de Lincy),* are three in number; and strongly resemble, as well in the gifts which they present to the child, as in their appearance and properties, the Parcæ of Classical, and the Norns of Scandinavian, Mythology. These last, again, figure under the name of " Elves" in Layamon's translation of the " Brut Chronicle: " where we learn—that, on the birth of Arthur—

Sone swa he com an eorthe	So soon he came on earth
Alven hine ivengen.	Elves received him.
Heo bigolen that child	They enchanted that child
Mid galdere swithe stronge.	With magic most strong.
Heo zeven him mihte	They gave him might
To beon best alre cnihten.	To be best of all knights.
Heo zeven him an other thing	They gave him another thing
That he scolde beon riche king.	That he should be a rich king.
Heo ziven him that thridde	They gave him the third
That he scolde longe libben.	That he should long live.
Heo ziven that kin-bern	They gave to that kingly child
Custen swithe gode.	Virtues most good.
That he was mete-custi	That he was most generous
Of alle quikemonnen, ·	Of all men alive,
This the Alven him zef.	This the Elves him gave.

Layamon, vv. 19254—19269.

Sir Frederick Madden, from whose admirable edition † of this valuable relic of our early literature we

---

* In his very interesting "Livre des Légendes," Introduction: —a work which makes us regret that the volumes, to which it was to serve as an introduction, have not yet been given to the world.

† Layamon's " Brut, or Chronicle of Britain; a Poetical Semi-Saxon Paraphrase of the Brut of Wace. Now first published

have taken the foregoing quotation, in remarking that
this curious passage is not in Wace—who contents
himself with stating,

> " Ertur son nom ; de sa bunté
> Ad grant parole puis esté "—

adds, " It will be remarked that the *Elves* in Layamon
bear a greater affinity to the *Fays of romance* than to
the *popular Fairies,* between whom is a marked difference." How far Sir F. Madden is justified in the
opinion which he advances in the latter part of the
same note—namely, that " It is almost certain that
the French received their knowledge of those *Fays*
from the Northern Mythology, in which the attendance of certain *Norns* or Fairies at the birth of a child
was recognized,"—we are not prepared to say.

From a consideration of the facts which have been
already adduced, and which might readily be mul-
tiplied a hundred-fold, it is obvious that while a confusion of names has led to a confusion of attributes,
the converse of that proposition is equally true, and
the well-known circumstance that different systems
of mythology ascribe certain given powers and offices
to beings of a character originally totally distinct, has
equally contributed to the confusion which now prevails in our Fairy Mythology :—in short, that a community of attributes has led to an interchange of
names.

I have entered at some length into these preliminary
observations on the intermixture of the superstitions
of different races discoverable in our fairy mythology,

---

from the Cottonian Manuscripts in the British Museum, accompanied by a Literal Translation, Notes, and a Grammatical
Glossary. By Sir Frederick Madden."

because, although it is probable that in no branch of our Folk-Lore will this intermixture be found to prevail to such an extent as in that which relates to Elves and Fairies, no division of the subject will be found entirely free from it: and because, before the reader proceeds to consider the various points in that fairy mythology to which Shakespeare's allusions must direct inquiry—the various attributes of fays and elves which, recorded by his immortalizing pen, have been fortunately perpetuated for the investigation of the antiquary,—it is essential that the reader's mind should be impressed with the fact, that the system which he is about to consider is not the immediate offspring of that which prevailed

> " In olde days of the King Artour
>   Of which that Bretons speken great honour,"

—nor of that which the followers of Hengist and Horsa spread amongst us ; but an intermixture of all these—that it possesses a many-sided character. In short, it is necessary to convince him of what the prejudiced view of the antiquary has too often dis-regarded,—namely, that the history of our superstitions, like that of our language and institutions, has to be traced back, not to the time of the Norman Conquest only—not even to the time of the Heptarchy—not even to the day when

> " Jove's bird, the Roman Eagle, winged
>   From the spungy south to this part of the west"—

but through the period when

> " A Roman and a British ensign waved
>   Friendly together, "

up to the very earliest ages of British history.

Archæology, in all its branches, is at length assum-

D

ing the precision of a science; and, reversing the rule which formerly prevailed, now seeks diligently for facts instead of endeavouring to supply their place by theories, and to make up by prejudice what may be wanting in knowledge.

The words of one of the most profound scholars of the present day will bring these remarks to a fitting close. Although originated by his inquiries into the etymology of Saxon boundaries, they will be found to apply most forcibly to the various phases of English Folk-Lore:—

"It cannot be doubted," says Mr. Kemble, "that local names, and those devoted to distinguish the natural features of a country, possess an inherent vitality which even the urgency of conquest is frequently unable to destroy. A race is rarely so entirely removed as not to form an integral, though subordinate, part of the new state based upon its ruins; and in the case where the cultivator continues to be occupied with the soil, a change of master will not necessarily lead to the abandonment of the names by which the land itself, and the instruments or processes of labour are designated. On the contrary, the conquering race are apt to adopt these names from the conquered; and thus after the lapse of twelve centuries and innumerable civil convulsions, the principal words of the class described yet prevail in the language of our people, and partially in our literature. Many, then, of the words which we seek in vain in the Anglo-Saxon dictionaries are, in fact, to be sought in those of the Cymri,—from whose practice they were adopted by the victorious Saxons in all parts of the country. They are not Anglo-Saxon, but Welsh (*i.e.*, Foreign Wylisc) very frequently unmodified either in meaning or pronunciation."

II. SHAKESPEARE'S ELVES AND FAIRIES.

" Fairies, black, grey, green and white,
    You moonshine revellers, and shades of night,
    You orphan–heirs of fixed destiny,
    Attend your office, and your quality."

THE most successful attempt which has hitherto been made to preserve the popular stories that are still current in any part of the British Islands is, unquestionably, " The Fairy Legends and Traditions of the South of Ireland," by Mr. Crofton Croker; and the reader who is interested in the " small philosophy " supposed to be involved in the study of popular superstitions will, doubtless, remember the curious essay " On the Nature of the Elves " written by the Brothers Grimm,—a translation of which forms so interesting a portion of the third volume of Mr. Croker's amusing work.

The writings of Shakespeare, and the records which he has left us of the sayings and doings, the haunts and habits, of our English

" Urchins, ouphes, and fairies green and white,"

furnish a poetical and striking commentary upon that learned dissertation,—as also upon the notes on the same subject which James Grimm has collected in his " German Mythology." For instance, one of the most striking peculiarities which the fairies of Shakespeare exhibit is their diminutive size.   Queen Mab

" comes
In shape no bigger than an agate stone
On the forefinger of an alderman ; "

and Puck tells us that when Oberon and Titania meet,

> " They square, that all the elves for fear
> Creep into acorn cups, and hide them there."

This corresponds exactly with the tiny dimensions attributed to them in the mythology of the north; where it is said, that men are of a middle size—between the giants and elves—the stature of the giants being as much greater than that of human beings as the stature of the elves is below it.*

The dwarf-like form of the elves is, however, variously described. They are sometimes represented as being of the size of a child of four years old. Thus Elberich, the most renowned of the dwarfs (the Oberon of Shakespeare be it remembered—but of this more hereafter,) is described, when discovered by Otnit sleeping under the linden tree, as being of the measure of a child of four years old,†

> "Nu bist in kindes mâze des vierden jahres alt."

And it is said of Antilois in Ulrich's "Alexander:" " Er was kleine und niht groz in der mâze als diu kint, wen si *in vier jâren* sint."—" He was little and not greater in measure than the child when it is in its fourth year."‡ When, therefore, Shakespeare makes

---

* Grimm, "Deutsche Mythologie," s. 418.

† Ettmuller's "Kunec Ortnides Mervart und Tot," ii. 24. Grimm, "Deutsche Mythologie," s. 418, remarks in a note that in the Middle Ages, the diminutive form ascribed to the dwarfs and elves was thence also attributed to the Christian angels. Thus we read in the Titurel of Wolfram von Eschenbach— " Ein jegelich *engel* schinet also gestalter als ein kint in *jaren vieren* in der jugende."

‡ Sir Joshua Reynolds little thought, at that happy moment

Mrs. Page, in compliance with the suggestion of her husband,

> "to make us public sport,
> Appoint a meeting with the fat old fellow,"

propose that

> "Nan Page, my daughter, and my little son,
> And three or four more of their growth, we'll dress
> Like urchins, ouphes, and fairies green and white,
> With rounds of waxen tapers on their heads
> And rattles in their hands,"

it is obvious that in the popular mind of England, at the time when he wrote "The Merry Wives of Windsor," the fairies were supposed sometimes to resemble little children, at least in size.

At other times, again, the stature of the elves is described, both in England and on the Continent, as being far beneath that ever assumed by mortals. Thus, the troop of fairies who appeared to Herman von Rosenberg when he was celebrating his nuptials, to request that they might at the same time hold the bridal feast of a newly married elfin-couple, are represented as having been scarcely "two spans" high; *—while the sprite (*wihtel*) mentioned in a fragment of "Gawain," printed by Hoffman von Fallersleben

---

of inspiration when he transferred to his glowing canvas the elfin and changing features of

> "that shrewd and knavish sprite
> Called Robin Goodfellow,"

what great authority he had for so representing that "tricksy spirit;" for giving that "merry wanderer of the night" the form of a little child—a form which we believe he has ever since assumed, in the minds of all who have once looked upon that beautiful creation of Sir Joshua's pencil.

* Grimm, "Deutsche Sagen," i. 54.

in the "Alt-Deutsche Blatter," is stated to have been
scarcely a *thumb* long—

> "Reht als ein doum elle
> Chum was er so lang!"*

These, therefore, approach far more closely to the
standard of Titania's followers; and might well have
taken part in the duties which she imposed upon her
train when she bade them—

> "Some, to kill cankers in the musk-rose buds,
> Some, war with rear mice for their leathern wings
> To make my small elves coats; and some keep back
> The clamorous owl that nightly hoots and wonders
> At our quaint spirits;"

and have joined Peasblossom, Cobweb, Moth, and
Mustard-seed in attendance upon Bottom, when
Titania commanded them—

> "Be kind and courteous to this gentleman;
> Hop in his walks, and gambol in his eyes;
> Feed him with apricots and dewberries
> With purple grapes, green figs, and mulberries;
> The honey bags steal from the humble bees,
> And for night-tapers crop their waxen thighs,
> And light them at the fiery glowworm's eyes
> To have my love to bed and to arise;
> And pluck the wings from painted butterflies,
> To fan the moonbeams from his sleeping eyes;
> Nod to him, elves, and do him courtesies."

That the belief in the existence of an elfin race
small enough to "creep into acorn-cups and hide
them there"† was not confined to this country, but

---

* We may here remark that the Elfin character of our *Tom
Thumb*—(the German *Dummling*, and the French *Petit Poucet*,)
which Grimm has somewhere noticed as being clearly indicated
by the intelligence with which he is gifted as well as by his
diminutive size, is as obviously pointed at in his name.

† Drayton, in his "Nymphidia," has a similar incident; his

was equally prevalent in Denmark, we learn from the
ballad of Éline of Villenskov, where it is said—

> "Out then spake the smallest Trold:
> *No bigger than an ant;*—
> Oh, here is come a Christian man,
> His schemes I'll sure prevent." *

We will not now stop to consider, with Grimm,
the circumstance that this tiny race is everywhere

---

elaborate description of which serves to mark, still more distinctly, the very minute size of his fairies :—

> "At length one chanced to find a nut,
> In th'end of which a hole was cut,
> Which lay upon a hazel root,
>   There scattered by a squirrel,
> Which out the kernel gotten had,
> When quoth this fay, ' Dear queen, be glad,
> Let Oberon be ne'er so mad
>   I'll set you safe from peril.'

> ' Come all into this nut,' quoth she,
> ' Come closely in—be ruled by me,
> Each one may here a chuser be,
>   For room, ye need not wrestle,
> Nor need ye be together heapt.'
> So one by one therein they crept,
> And lying down, they soundly slept,
>   And safe as in a castle."

It is a curious fact, that next to Shakespeare we are indebted
to Drayton, another Warwickshire man, for the best materials
for our fairy mythology. Is that country still rich in fairy-
lore ?—and if so, will no one undertake the pleasant task of
collecting it ?

* Danske Viser, I. 176.

> "Det da meldte den mindste Trold
>   Han var ikke storre end en myre ;
> Her er kommet en Christen mand,
>   Den maa jeg visseligen styre."

represented as forming a nation of themselves; a fact
which has led some antiquaries to believe that in
certain regions at least, if not in all, the traditions of
the fairy or elfin race have reference to a people sub-
jugated by a nation whose descendants now inhabit
such districts.   When Shakespeare's allusions to the
King and Queen of Fairy Land shall be under consideration, some observations respecting the people
over whom they rule may find more fitting place.

Turn we, in the meanwhile, to the subject of their
inordinate love of music and dancing.   There is
scarcely any one point in the fairy character upon
which the universal voice of national tradition is so
well agreed, as upon that which relates to the fondness everywhere exhibited by the fairies for music
and revelry.   To them, according to the legendary
records of every country, is owing such mysterious
and harmonious sounds as Caliban describes when he
says—

> "The isle is full of noises ;
> Sounds and sweet airs, that give delight and harm not.
> Sometimes a thousand twangling instruments
> Will hum about mine ears ; and sometimes voices
> That, if I then had waked after long sleep,
> Will make me sleep again ;"

and in like manner does the Folk-Lore of every nation
abound in well-remembered instances of their being
seen to meet—

> "On hill, in dale, forest, or mead,
>   By paved fountain, or by rushy brook,
>   Or on the beached margent of the sea,
>   To dance their ringlets to the whistling wind."

The writings of Shakespeare abound in graphic
notices of these fairy revels, couched in the highest

strains of poetry; and a comparison of these with
some of the popular legends which the industry of
continental antiquaries has preserved will show us
clearly, that these delightful sketches of elfin enjoy-
ment have been drawn by a hand as faithful as it is
masterly. As the object of these papers, however, is
to illustrate the writings of Shakespeare, rather than
to quote them, one brilliant passage from the close of
the " Midsummer Night's Dream "—which proves
that, even when bestowing a blessing upon mortals,
the fairies oftentimes accompanied their precious gifts
by both " a Roundel and a Fairy Song "—will show
how he made use of the popular belief of his own time
and country as the machinery of his dramas, and how
closely that belief corresponds with the traditions of
many of the other nations of Europe—

> " *Puck.* And we fairies, that do run
> By the triple Hecat's team
> From the presence of the sun,
>   Following darkness like a dream,
> Now are frolic ; not a mouse
> Shall disturb this hallowed house :
> I am sent with broom before
> To sweep the dust behind the door.
>   (*Enter Oberon and Titania with all their Train.*)
> *Oberon.* Through the house give glimmering light
>   By the dead and drowsy fire ;
> Every elf, and fairy sprite,
>   Hop as light as bird from brier ;
>   And this ditty after me
>   Sing, and dance it trippingly.
> *Titania.* First, rehearse your song by rote,
>   To each word a warbling note.
>   Hand in hand, with fairy grace,
>   Will we sing and bless this place."

If the reader would learn how far the fairies are

indebted for this love of music and dancing to a
taste which they may have inherited from their Celtic
progenitors, let him turn to the popular traditions of
Brittany, which tell how the Korrigans or Dwarfs
are there seen, night after night, dancing their merry
rounds to the twinkling stars; and that the burden
of their song or roundel was originally *"Monday,
Tuesday, Wednesday,"*—to which *" Thursday and
Friday "* have, more recently, been added: while
"Saturday and Sunday," being to them days marked
with a black stone, have never been allowed to form
a portion of the elfin chorus.* Schreiber tells us,
however,† that a midnight wanderer, who accidentally
intruded upon their revelry, tired of so monotonous
a song, varied it by adding the fatal words *"Saturday
and Sunday;"* but that no sooner had he given utter-
ance to them, than he was pinched, kicked, and cuffed
by the tiny host, until he was left half dead upon the
plain. Whereas, had he concluded the song, as he
ought to have done, with the words *"And so ends the
week!"* the long repentance to which the Korrigans
are condemned would that moment have been brought
to a conclusion.‡ The Breton peasant who believes
and relates these legends cautions the wayfarer who

---

* Villemarqué, " Barzas-Breiz. Chants Populaires de la
Bretagne," tome i. p. 50.

† " Hexen und Feen," p. 38. The legend of Knockgrafton,
in Crofton Croker's " Fairy Legends," resembles this in many
particulars: and a Spanish story, to the same effect, is told in
Thoms' " Lays and Legends of Spain," p. 83.

‡ Maury, " Les Fées du Moyen Age," expresses his opinion,
that the belief in these nocturnal dances has its origin in those
rites of Druidism, as well as of the Polytheism of Greece and
Rome, which were celebrated at night: adding—Horace thus

may chance to hear the unearthly music of the Korrigans not to yield to the temptation of joining their mazy dances; and warns him that if he once does so, he will be dragged into the circle and compelled to dance until he drops and dies from exhaustion.

How bewitching is the music of the Welsh fairies, —how irresistible the desire to join their dance which it awakens in those who hear it—the melancholy fate of Rhys ap Morgan, as recorded by Davidd Shone, will serve to show us.[*]

Pluquet tells us, in his "Contes Populaires de Bayeux," that the fairy rings called by the peasants of Normandy *Cercles des Fées*, are believed by them to be formed by the fairies—

"Where round and round all nights, in moonshine fair,
They dance to some strange music in the air."

And Mdlle. Bosquet[†] confirms his statements. These Norman sprites may possibly be of Celtic descent; but the *Oennereeske,* or underground people of Friesic tradition, whose tiny footsteps are seen imprinted in the Dunes of Frieseland are, on the other hand, unquestionably of Scandinavian origin. Of their love of music and dancing there can be little doubt, since

---

represents Venus conducting the Chorus of Dancers beneath the pale beams of the watery moon :—

"Jam Cytherea choros ducit Venus, imminente Lunâ,
Junctæque Nymphis Gratiæ decentes."—*Lib.* i. *Od.* 4."

[*] "Fairy Mythology of the South of Ireland," vol. iii., p. 214.

[†] "La Normandie Romanesque et Merveilleuse." Grimm, "Deutsche Mythologie," p. 438, informs us that these circlets are called *Alledands* by the Danes, and *Alfdands* by the Swedes. We may add that the Norwegians designate them by a similar name—*Alfedands.*

Kohl* was assured that they sometimes joined the shepherds in their dances on the heath, and at other times were discovered sitting on barrows and tumuli, singing and playing instruments of music.

Faye gives a similar account of the fondness for dancing exhibited by the Norwegian elves: and if we turn to Thiele's " Danish Legends," we there meet with corresponding notices of the " elve folk " of Denmark; while Afzelius furnishes similar records of the Swedish elves.

To these latter is attributed the same jealousy of mortal eye espying their wild revelry which made Falstaff exclaim —

> " They are fairies; he that speaks to them shall die !
> I'll wink and couch ; no man their work must eye."

And the ballad of " Sir Olof," one of the most popular in the rich ballad literature of Sweden and Denmark, turns upon this peculiarity of the fairy character. The following is a translation from a version given by Arrwiddson in his " Svenska Fornsanger: " †

Sir Olof and the Fairies.

> Sir Olof rides out at break of day,
> *Falling the dew and driving the mist,*
> He rides till he reaches the mountain grey,
> *At even Sir Olof returns again.*

---

* Kohl, " Die Marschen und Inseln der Herzogthumer Schleswig und Holstein," ii. 267.

† " Svenska Fornsanger, En Samling af Kampavisor, Folk Visor, Lekar och Dansar, samt Barn och Vall-Sanger," 3 vols. 8vo. This admirable collection of Swedish popular songs is far less known in this country than it deserves to be. The learned editor, Adolf Iwar Arwiddson, is the Librarian of the Royal Library at Stockholm.

E'er Sir Olof had ridden that mountain o'er,
  Falling the dew, &c.,
The Elf-King's daughter stood him before,
  At even Sir Olof, &c.

Her snowy white hand outstretched she,
" Oh, prithee, Sir Olof, come dance with me."

" With thee, maiden, dance, I nor can nor may,
For to-morrow it is my bridal day."

That elf-maiden smote with her hand so white,
" Sorrow and sickness on thee alight ! "

That elf-maiden smote with her cap so small,
" No more shall priest's benison on thee fall ! "

Sir Olof has turned his noble steed,
And home to his mother has ridden with speed.

And straight when she saw him that mother said,
" What has paled that cheek, once so bonny and red ? "

" Oh well may my cheek so pale be found,
For, alas ! I have trodden on fairy ground.

" To-morrow my love with her maidens will come
To ask thee, oh mother, why tarrieth thy son.

" And when she thus asks thee, oh mother, then say,
My son to the greenwood hath taken his way."

When the night it was past, and the day it was come,
Came his love and her bridesmaids to Sir Olof's home.

" God's blessing, oh mother-in-law, rest on thee,
Say, where is my bridegroom, say where tarrieth he ? "

" Askest thou after Olof, thy bridegroom so gay,
My son to the greenwood hath taken his way."

" O say, does he prize more the hart and the roe
Than the love of his young bride, oh can it be so ? "

Then straightway she goes to his chamber so wide,
The arras and hanging she throweth aside,

Then straightway she draweth the curtains so red,
And there lay Sir Olof, but Sir Olof lay dead.

And when from that chamber the maiden came down,
Her fair hair hung wildly beneath her gold crown.

And before the next morning's sun arose,
There were three lying dead in Sir Olof's house.

The first was Sir Olof, the second his bride,
  Falling the dew and driving the mist,
The third was his mother, for sorrow she died.
  At even Sir Olof returns again.

We will bring the present paper to a close with a
Flemish Legend; which, while it exhibits another
instance of fairy fondness for music and dancing, (for,
doubtless, the merry dancers therein were fairies,) will
serve at the same time to show the uncertainty and
capriciousness of the elfin character.

An old fiddler was returning home from the fair at
Opbrakel,—where he had contrived to line his purse
pretty well by the exercise of his calling; and his
road lay through the Forest of Nederbrakel, in the
neighbourhood of which he resided. It was just midnight; and Kartof—for such was the fiddler's name—
who had learned from the Americans to love the
fragrant weed, felt how much he should enjoy the
company of his pipe if he could but get a light. By
great good luck, just as this wish arose in his mind,
he perceived a light in the middle of the wood. He
accordingly turned his steps in that direction; and
on reaching the spot whence the light proceeded, was
surprised to see a glorious bonfire and a number of
men and women dancing around it. Kartof begged
the favour of a light; and twenty hands were instantly
stretched out to supply his want. Well pleased was

the old fiddler when he found his pipe once more
alight, and the grateful vapour curling round his
nostrils. While he was taking a few quiet whiffs
before resuming his journey, one of the dancers spied
the violin under his arm; and begged him, in return
for their civility, to play a few dance tunes. To
this, Kartof, who was a little vain of his skill, readily
consented; and while he was tuning his instrument
they handed him a glass of capital wine by way of
encouraging him to do his best. At length all was
ready. Kartof struck up one of his liveliest airs,—
and off went the dancers: and so well pleased were
they with his performance, that they kept ever and
anon rewarding him with bright gold-pieces, and
plying him with the good liquor to keep his strength
up. After some time, the wine and the exertion of
playing overpowered poor Kartof, and he dropped
down upon the grass fast asleep;—and so the dance
ended. The sun was high in the heavens, next
morning, when Kartof awoke, and lifted his heavy
head from the ground to see where he had been
sleeping and to collect his scattered senses. He found
himself in the middle of the wood, beside a heap
of ashes which were still smouldering. He tried
his fiddle; for his drunkenness had not made him for-
get his performance of the preceding night—nor the
rich guerdon which he had received for it. His fiddle
was all right; but when he came to look at the gold
pieces—oh, misery and disappointment!—they were
all turned to beech leaves, the same as those which
lay around him in thousands. So, poor Kartof returned home, with an aching head and a troubled
spirit—sorely puzzled what to make of his adven-
tures in the Forest of Nederbrakel.

III. Puck, or Robin Goodfellow.

"My gentle Puck, come hither."

N the brilliant and animated picture which Shakespeare has left us of the Court of Fairy, its pomps and revelry, crowded as the canvas is with objects of beauty and interest, there is one figure which stands so prominently forward as instantly to arrest our attention—one figure on which, unmindful of the gorgeous imagery by which it is surrounded, the eye delights to dwell. It is not that of "jealous Oberon, captain of the fairy band"—it is not that of "proud Titania"—but it is the well-drawn and richly-coloured portrait of

> "that shrewd and knavish sprite
> Called Robin Goodfellow."

And the object of the present paper is to show that, masterly as is the portrait as a work of Art, there is not one touch in it which is not based in truth. In the character of Puck Shakespeare has embodied almost every attribute with which the imagination of the people has invested the Fairy race; and has neither omitted one trait necessary to give brilliancy and distinctness to the likeness, nor sought to heighten its effect by the slightest exaggeration. For, carefully and elaborately as he has finished the picture, he has not in it invested the " Lob of Spirits " with one gift or quality which the popular voice of the age was not unanimous in bestowing upon him. What those gifts, powers, and qualities were, let Shakespeare tell us :—

" *Fairy.* Either I mistake your shape and making quite,
Or else you are that shrewd and knavish sprite
Call'd Robin Goodfellow. Are you not he,
That frights the maidens of the villagery;
Skims milk; and sometimes labours in the quern;
And bootless makes the breathless housewife churn;
And sometimes makes the drink to bear no barm;
Misleads night-wanderers, laughing at their harm.
Those that Hobgoblin call you, and sweet Puck,
You do their work, and they shall have good luck;
Are you not he?
    Puck.   Thou speak'st aright.
I am that merry wanderer of the night.
I jest to Oberon, and make him smile,
When I a fat and bean-fed horse beguile,
Neighing in likeness of a filly foal:
And sometimes lurk I in a gossip's bowl,
In very likeness of a roasted crab;
And when she drinks against her lips I bob,
And on her wither'd dewlap pour the ale.
The wisest aunt telling the saddest tale,
Sometimes for three-foot stool mistaketh me;
Then slip I from her bum, down topples she,
And " Tailor " cries, and falls into a cough:
And then the old quire hold their hips and laugh,
And waxen in their mirth, and neeze, and swear,
A merrier hour was never wasted there."

The speech which Puck makes to fright the " crew
of patches "—

" I'll follow you, I'll lead you about, around,
   Through bog, through bush, through brake, through brier,
   Sometime a horse I'll be, sometime a hound;
   A hog, a headless bear, sometime a fire;
And neigh, and bark, and grunt, and roar, and burn,
Like horse, hound, hog, bear, fire, at every turn;"

and that in which he describes the trick that he has
put upon Bottom—

      " An ass's nowl I fixed on his head,"

complete this masterly sketch. Let us analyze it, and

we shall see how admirably and consistently has the imagination of Shakespeare, while thus " bodying forth the form of things unknown," incorporated in this one picture in little, all the characteristics of the elfin race as they were preserved in the " Folk-Lore " of his day.   And that this was done designedly and of aforethought can scarcely be doubted, when it is borne in mind that Shakespeare has designated this personification of the fairy tribe not by any imaginary title, but simply as Puck.   For though " Puck " is now only applied to designate the " merry wanderer of the night," it was originally a name applied to the whole race of fairies,* and not to any individual sprite.   Nay, more, it is the name by which they are still designated by the peasantry of Friesland and Jutland ; and when we remember how large a proportion of what are called our Anglo-Saxon progenitors migrated from those countries, it seems scarcely too much to say, with M. Kohl, " that the Jutes and Anglo-Saxons could not even get rid of the Pucks when they sailed for England."

Be this as it may, however, it will at least justify us in applying the curious information which this amusing traveller has collected on the subject of these Friesian sprites to illustrate the history and character of our own " sweet Puck." Puk, Nis Puk, Huispuk, Niskepuk, Wolterke, Nisebok, Nisske, Nisskuke, and Pulter Claas, are the names which are applied in those regions, according to the statement of Kohl,† to the

---

* More upon this point, when the curious subject of the names by which the fairies are designated in the writings of Shakespeare shall come under our consideration.

† " Die Marschen und Inseln der Herzogthumer Schleswig und Holstein," von J. G. Kohl, band ii., s. 282, et seq.

domestic or household spirit. Of these Puk, or Niss Puk, is that which is most commonly bestowed upon him, as well by the Friesians as by the Jutes and Danes. And in every way, continues that writer, is the name of this spirit most remarkable, since it is the same under which he passed over into England, where he plays the same pranks as on this side of the Northern Ocean, and where those pranks have been sung and celebrated by the greatest poet of that nation. What Shakespeare has so poetically related of the tricks and merry pranks of Puck is told at the present day, only somewhat more coarsely, by the peasantry of Friesland and Jutland.

The Puks, like the *Oennereeske*, or underground people, are small and dwarflike. They are described as wearing pointed red caps, long grey or green jackets, and slippers on their feet. They take up their abode under the roof, whither they go in and out at pleasure, either through a broken window, which no one ventures to mend, or through some other opening left for the purpose. As the Romans made offerings to their Lares, and prepared food for them, so the Friesians set out on the floor a bowl of porridge for the Puk, who is not well pleased if it be not made more palatable by a bit of butter.* Although people generally feel a certain dread of these Puks, and do not very readily approach the places which they are known to frequent, these spirits are on the whole well disposed towards mankind, and anxious to be on good terms with them. For, like

---

* Kohl adds, " The same custom is observed in the Erzge-birge at the present day; and the Letts, Cossaks, and other people say it was formerly practised among them."

the *Oennereeske,* the Puks are of themselves neither decidedly malicious nor beneficent. When pleased with the master of the house in which they reside, they take upon themselves at night the performance of all the household duties*—wash and cleanse the rooms and furniture, bring in fodder, tend the cattle, and take care that everything thrives. Nay, so anxious are they that it should be so, that rather than fail they do not scruple to rob the neighbours. They are oftentimes heard in the middle of the night bustling over their work, and going up and down about the house; and sometimes they amuse themselves by playing tricks upon the maids and servants, tickling them under the nose to make them sneeze in their sleep, pulling off the bed-clothes, and indulging in such other pranks as those which Shakespeare attributes to his celebrated Queen Mab. The tricks played by these Puks upon the goodman of the house are oftentimes of so comic a character that one can scarcely conceive how they ever entered into the imagination of the people.

They tell a story of one of these Puks, who was once seen, in broad daylight, sitting outside a garret window, with his head resting idly on both hands, and who amused himself by singing the praise of his own beauty, although he was frightfully ugly, and

---

* So, in the very remarkable account of the domestic spirit *Hinzelman* which Grimm has given in his "Deutsche Sagen," i., p. 103, et seq., we find that precisely the same description of household duties was undertaken by that drudging fiend; and other stories in the same collection furnish similar instances. Thiele furnishes legends of the same character from Denmark; Crofton Croker from Ireland; and Chambers gives us a corresponding account of the Scottish Brownie.

the roundness and symmetry of his legs, which he kept bobbing up and down, although those legs were as thin as sticks; and thus he continued, now teazing the yard-dog by holding out to him first one and then the other of his shrivelled legs, and now mocking the servants and making faces at them, until at last one of the stable-boys crept up stealthily behind him, and with a pitchfork pushed him down off the window sill. But down into the yard Puk never fell, for nothing reached the ground but some broken potsherds and dirty straw. Puk was, however, greatly offended at the trick which had been played him, and soon took his revenge.

When these Puks are offended with the master of the house, they plague him so incessantly, and play him so many tricks, that he is at last fain to abandon his house. Yet it often happens that he does not, by so doing, get freed from his domestic spirit; for, like the " *atra cura* " of Horace, the Puks continue to follow him, let him take as much pains as he may to keep his plans a secret from them. They conceal themselves in the waggon in which his household goods are packed up; and when, on the journey, they are discovered, and asked " What are you doing here?" they repeat the answer which the peasant had given to the inquiries of his neighbours—" Oh! we are moving to-day."* Thus, the Jutes and Anglo-

---

* Crofton Croker, in the notes to his story of the " Haunted Cellar " (" Fairy Legends of the South of Ireland," i., p. 143) has collected several amusing instances of the failure of such attempts to get rid of these domestic spirits; and Grimm, in his " Deutsche Sagen," i., p. 93, relates a story of a peasant who, driven to desperation by the tricks of a Kobold, determined, by way of getting rid of him, to burn the barn in which the spirit

Saxons could not free themselves from the Puks when they crossed the seas to England, for they followed them thither.

How striking is the resemblance between this account of the manner in which the Friesian peasant

> " Tells how the drudging Goblin sweat
> To earn his cream-bowl duly set "

and that of our own sweet Puck! Their names are not more identical than their characteristics. For as the Friesian Puk when kindly disposed would, we see, do the work and give good luck to those who pleased him, so, on the other hand, he was as ready as our own hobgoblin "to fright the maidens of the villagery,"

> " And bootless make the breathless housewife churn."

The manner in which Puck's favour was bestowed on those "that Hobgoblin called him and sweet Puck" is also faithfully copied from popular belief as it exists in these islands as well as on the Continent. Thus, in Germany the favour of the elves is propitiated by bestowing on them such a name as *Gutgesell, nachbar,* or *lieber nachbar;* and in the Netherlands, *goede kind*—in Denmark, *gad dreng, kiarre granne,* are names bestowed upon them with the same object. In Ireland, again, they are called *the good people;* in Scotland, *the good neighbours;*

---

had taken up its abode. Accordingly, having removed his corn from it, he set fire to the Kobold's retreat ; and, when the flames were at their height, was just congratulating himself upon being freed from his tormentor, when he heard his well-known voice calling out from the waggon on which he was removing his property—" It was quite time for us to come out ! It was quite time for us to come out !"

and Mr. Chambers* tells us that in the latter country
" the fairies are said to have been exceedingly sensi-
tive upon the subjects of their popular appellations.
They considered the term " Fairy " disreputable, and
are thought to have pointed out their approbation
and disapprobation of the other phrases applied to
them in the following verses :—

> " Gin ye ca' me imp or elf,
> I rede ye look weel to yourself;
> Gin ye ca' me fairy,
> I'll work you muckle tarrie (*vexation*);
> Gin gude neibor ye ca' me,
> Then gude neibor I will be;
> But gin ye ca' me seelie wicht,
> I'll be your friend both day and nicht."

And Kirk, in his " Secret Commonwealth "—one of
the most curious treatises on any subject connected
with popular mythology ever penned—tells us,
" These *Siths* or fairies they call *Sleagh Maith*, or the
Good People, it would seem to prevent the dint of
their ill-attempts—(for the Irish use to bless all they
fear harm of)." In the characters, too, which Puck
assumes when his object is to

> " Mislead night wanderers, laughing at their harm,"

—for which purpose he says,

> " Sometime a horse I'll be, sometime a hound,
> A hog, a headless bear, sometime a fire,"

—he is, as unquestionably, only taking upon himself
forms which the spirits of popular belief were con-

---

* In page 32 (edit. 1842) of his very valuable, because
obviously genuine, collection of Scottish Folk-Lore, entitled
" Popular Rhymes, Fireside Stories and Amusements of Scotland."

stantly in the habit of assuming.   How very ancient
and far-spread is the belief in spirits, or fairies, assuming the form of a horse, we learn from Gervase of
Tilbury; who, in a well-known and oft-quoted passage of his " Otia Imperialia," speaks of a spirit which
in England was called *Grant,** and appeared in
" likeness of a filly foal."   " Est in Angliâ quoddam
demonum genus, quod suo idiomate *Grant* nominant
ad instar pulli equini anniculi," &c.; and Mr. Keightley, in his " Fairy Mythology," has shown from Grose
" that in Hampshire they still give the name of Colt
Pixy to a supposed spirit, or fairy, which, in the shape
of a horse, *wickers*, i.e., neighs and misleads horses
into bogs," &c.—a prank which is exactly one of
those that Puck plays when he assumes the shape of
a horse " to make Oberon smile."   Pluquet, in describing Le Goubelin or gobelin of Normandy—who
resembles Shakespeare's Puck in many particulars—
tells us, among other things, that he sometimes takes
the form of a handsome black horse,—but, woe to
the unhappy traveller who is tempted to bestride
him! and we learn from Mdlle. Bosquet that *Le
Chevalier Bayard* is the name given to this Lutin or
gobelin by the Norman peasantry.   I have printed
in the " Lays and Legends of Spain," p. 93, a curious
account of a spirit horse, extracted from Torque-
meda's " Spanish Mandeville of Miracles"; and also
another extract from the same work, in which is an
account of " two great black mastives"—which are

---

* Grimm, " Deutsche Mythologie," ss. 222 and 946, points
out the resemblance between this name and that of the malicious spirit *Grendel* in Beowulf. Grimm alludes also to the
fact, as connected with this subject, that the Devil is represented
in many places as being discoverable by his horse-foot.

òbviously evil spirits who have assumed that appearance.

This, then, is an authority, and one of which frequent instances might be adduced, for Puck's assumption of the form of a "hound." But the consideration of spirits in the form of hounds would almost form a chapter of itself. We will therefore pass that by for the present; as also that of Puck's self-transformation into a fire—by which, although it is not expressly stated, it is clear that Shakespeare alluded to the *Will-o'-the-Wisp*. Grimm furnishes some instances of the Evil One assuming the shape of a "hog"; and, as in the transformations which Puck assumes the more malevolent features of the elfin character are discoverable, such instances as the present serve to show how, in the ever-varying phases of the popular mythology, the once harmless fairies have gradually got confounded with the spirit of evil—a state of things to which the introduction of Christianity has no doubt greatly contributed.

What authority Shakespeare had for making his shrewd and knavish sprite take upon himself the shape of a bear I know not. Some such authority will no doubt be discovered. But the only connection between elves and bears which I remember to have met with is in the following Norwegian legend,*—a counterpart of which may very possibly have been current in England when Shakespeare wrote, and so have suggested to him the transformation in question.

---

* A High German poetical version of this legend occurs in a MS. of the fourteenth century pieserved at Heidelberg. An analytical translation of it will be found in Grimm's "Essay on the Elves." in Croker's "Fairy Legends," iii., p. 131, et seq.

There was once a man up in Finmark, who had caught a great white bear, which he determined to take as a present to the King of Denmark. Now, it fell out, that while he was on his journey, he arrived on Christmas Eve at the village of Dovrefield; and accident brought him to the house of a man named Halvor, of whom he begged a night's lodging for himself and his bear. " Ah! God help me," exclaimed Halvor, " how can I give anybody a night's lodging? Why every Christmas Eve I have so many Trolls (Elves) come to this house, that I and all my family are obliged to quit it, and have not even a roof to cover us."

" Oh, you may give me a shelter for all that," said the man; " for my bear can sleep here behind the stove, and I can creep into the bed-press."

Halvor had nothing to say against this; but he and his family withdrew,—taking care, however, to get everything ready for the Trolls, and to leave plenty of rice-milk, dried fish and sausages upon the tables, and, in fact, everything necessary to make them a good feast.

As soon as they were gone, in came the Trolls. Some were large, some little, some had long tails, some none, and some had monstrous noses; but all ate, and drank, and enjoyed the good things that were set before them. In the midst of their merriment, one of the little Trolls, who had espied the bear sleeping behind the stove, stuck a piece of sausage on the end of a fork, and holding it under the bear's nose, called out " Pussy, pussy, do you like sausage too?" Upon which the bear being roused and angered, began to growl so terribly that he soon frightened the Trolls, great and small, out of the house.

Next year, just before Christmas, when Halvor was in the forest chopping wood and making ready for a visit from the Trolls, he suddenly heard some one calling him by name, " Halvor, Halvor."—" Yes," said Halvor.—" Have you got your great cat still ?"—" Yes," said Halvor, " and she has got seven kittens fiercer and bigger than herself."—" Oh !" said the Troll, " if that's the case, we won't enter your doors again," and from that time forth Halvor was never troubled with the Trolls again on Christmas Eve.

IV.—PUCK AS WILL-O'-THE-WISP.

"Some call him Robin Goodfellow,
Hob-goblin, or Mad Crisp;
And some againe doe terme him oft
By name of *Will-the-Wispe*."

THAT we are justified in saying, it is clear that Shakespeare alluded to the Will-o'-the-Wisp when he makes Puck declare that, among other shapes, he will be " sometime a fire," is proved by other passages in his writings. The first, and the more obvious one, is that in which Stephano, after Ariel has led him and his drunken companions through

"Tooth'd briers, sharp furzes, pricking goss and thorns,"

and " left them i' the filthy mantled pool," reproaches Caliban : " Monster, your fairy, which you say is a harmless fairy, has done little better than play'd the Jack with us,"—that is, as Dr. Johnson observes, " He has played Jack-with-a-Lanthorn, has led us about like an Ignis fatuus, by which travellers are decoyed into the mire."

"The Tempest" contains another allusion to this
subject.   It is in the speech in which Ariel—who, it
must be remembered, is, like Puck, a fairy—assures
Prospero that he has

> "Performed to point, to every article,
>   The tempest that he bade him;"

and runs as follows:—

> "I boarded the King's ship; now on the beak,
>   Now in the waist, the deck, in every cabin,
>   I flam'd amazement: sometimes I'd divide,
>   And burn in many places: on the top mast,
>   The yards and bowsprits, would I flame distinctly;
>   Then meet and join; Jove's lightnings, the precursors
>   O' the dreadful thunder-claps, more momentary
>   And sight-outrunning were not."

A third passage, the peculiar force of which was
first pointed out by Mr. Hunter, in his recent and
valuable addition to our stores of Shakespearian
Illustration,* occurs in "Lear," where Gloster's torch
being seen in the distance, the Fool says, "Look,
here comes a walking fire."   Whereupon Edgar,
speaking in his assumed character, says, "This is the
foul fiend, Flibbertigibet; he begins at Curfew, and
walks till the first cock."   "From which," observes
Mr. Hunter, "Flibbertigibet seems to be a name for
the Will-o'-the-Wisp.   Hence the propriety of 'He
begins at Curfew, and walks till the crowing of the
cock;' that is, is seen in all the dark of night."

That Mr. Hunter is right is unquestionable, from
Mad Tom's previous declaration that he is one "whom
the foul fiend hath led through fire and through flame,

---

* "New Illustrations of the Life, Studies, and Writings of
Shakespeare," vol. ii., p. 272.

through ford and through whirlpool, over bog and quagmire." And it would only have been part of that consistency observable in the most trifling speech of every personage in Shakespeare's dramas that Edgar should avail himself, upon the mention of the " walking fire," to carry on his assumed character of Mad Tom, by identifying it with the "foul fiend" by whom he had been so grievously misled. But it is a curious fact, which has hitherto, I believe, escaped the notice of the commentators, that when Shakespeare wrote " *a walking fire* " was a common name for the Ignis fatuus, as we learn from the story "How Robin Goodfellow lead a Company of Fellowes out of their way."*

" A company of young men having beene making merry with their sweethearts, were, at their coming home, to come over a heath. Robin Goodfellow, knowing of it, met them, and to make some pastime hee led them up and downe the heathe a whole night, so that they could not get out of it, for hee went before them in the shape of *a walking fire,* which they all saw and followed till the day did appeare; then Robin left them, and at his departure spake these words :—

> " Get you home, you merry lads,
> Tell your mammies and your dads,
> And all those that newes desire,
> How you saw *a walking fire,*†

---

* See p. 21 of "The Mad Pranks and Merry Jests of Robin Goodfellow." Reprinted from the Edition of 1628, with an Introduction by J. Payne Collier, Esq., F.S.A.; not the least curious of the publications of the Percy Society, or of the many reprints, for which the admirers of our early literature are indebted to the zeal and acquirements of my excellent friend.

† So in the poetical chap-book called " The Merry Pranks of

> Wenches, that doe smile and lispe,
> Use to call me Willy-Wispe."

This quotation proves both that Lear's Fool supposed Gloster's torch to be a Will-o'the-Wisp, and also, what we desired to show, that Puck, or Robin Goodfellow, sometimes under such a form

> "Misled night-faring clowns
> O'er hills, and sinking bogs, and pathless downs."

The connection between the Ignis fatuus and the Elfin race has been noticed by Grimm, who remarks that it is pointed at in the earliest names for this walking light which he has met with, namely, *elflicht* and the Danish *Vættylis;* while the connection which subsists between the Ignis fatuus and the domestic spirits is shown by the fact that it is frequently designated after mankind, as Will-of-the-Wisp, Will-with-the-Wisp, Jack-o'-Lanthorn, &c.

The popular belief as to the nature of this appearance is divided at the present day—at least in Germany, where it is generally designated Irlicht or Irwish, from its similarity to a wisp (in German *wisch*) of lighted straw. According to some, these phantoms are believed to be the souls of children who have died unbaptized; while others again believe them to be the restless spirits of wicked and covetous men who have not scrupled, for the sake of their own aggrandisement, to " remove their neighbours' landmarks."

Robin Goodfellow, very pleasant and witty," reprinted by Mr. Collier, we read, p. xviii—

> " Sometimes he'd counterfeit a voyce,
> And travellers call astray ;
> Sometimes *a walking fire* he'd be,
> And lead them from their way."

In Brittany, as we learn from Villemarqué, the *Porte-brandon** appears in the form of a child bearing a torch, which he turns like a burning wheel; and with this it is said that he sets fire to the villages, which are sometimes suddenly in the middle of the night wrapped in flames.

In Lusatia, where these wandering wildfires are also supposed to be the souls of unbaptized children, they are believed to be perfectly harmless,† and to be relieved from their destined wanderings as soon as any pious hand throws a handful of consecrated ground after them.

The *Lygtemænd*, or Lightmen, of Denmark are the spirits of unjust men, who by holding out a false light seek to allure wayfarers into fens and other dangerous places. The best defence against them is for the party who sees them to turn his cap inside out.‡ Whoever sees them must take care not to point at them, otherwise they will come and do him a mischief. It is also said that when a Lygteman is called he will come and shine before the party who called him, but who must take care that he does not injure him for his presumption in so calling him.

In the parish of Juulstrup, near Aalborg, some

---

* "Barzas-Breiz," I. 230, where other particulars of this Breton *feu-follet* are recorded.

† Grave, "Volksagen und Volksthûmliche Denkmale der Lausitz," p. 167.

‡ In the interesting notice of the Pixies of Devonshire [*Ath.* 991], we are told that they delight in leading astray such persons as they find abroad after nightfall, and that the only remedy in such a case is to turn some part of the dress. So Bishop Corbet, in his "Iter Septentrionale"—

" turn your cloaks,
Said he, for Puck is busy in these oaks."

peasants were once packing corn in the middle of the night when it was pitch dark. Suddenly one of these spirits appeared, to whom a boy called out fearlessly —"You had better come and shine before us." Whereupon the Lygteman approached, settled over where they were loading, then followed with the waggon till it came right to the granary. Near Skovby by Falker these Lygtemen are very numerous. They are there said to be the ghosts of land surveyors, who in their lifetime have acted unjustly in their admeasurements, and are now condemned to run up the Hill of Skovby and measure it with red-hot iron rods, exclaiming while they do so, " This is a right and proper boundary, from here to here."[*] Afzelius relates a similar legend which is current in Sweden.[†]

Mdlle. Bosquet, in her " Normandie Romanesque et Merveilleuse," gives us some very curious notices upon the subject of the popular belief in Normandy regarding these Feux Follets. They are there regarded as cruel and malicious spirits, whom it is extremely dangerous to encounter. To fly from them is to invite them to follow and persecute the unhappy wight who sees them, whose only chance of escape is to throw himself on his face and invoke the Divine assistance in releasing him from his danger. Among the superstitions which prevail on this subject are two deserving of notice: one is that the Ignis fatuus is the spirit of some unhappy woman, who is destined thus to run *en fourolle* to expiate her intrigues with a minister of the church, and it is

---

* See Thiele " Danmarks Folkesagn," ii. 299.
† Swenska Folkets Sago-Hafder, ii. 172.

designated from that circumstance La Fourlore or La Fourolle. Another opinion is, that Le Feu Follet is the soul of a priest who has been condemned thus to expiate his broken vows of perpetual chastity; and it is very probable that it is to some similar belief existing in this country at the time when he wrote that Milton alludes in L'Allegro, when he says,—

> " She was pinched and pulled, she said,
> And he by Friars' Lanthorn led."

In the curious collection which Kuhn has published under the title of " Märkische Sagen und Legenden " we find two passages which serve to illustrate the preceding notices. The first, particularly, will show that it was consistent with the elfin character of Puck that he should assume the form of the Will-of-the-Wisp. It is the legend of a peasant in Schwina, who for a long time had a Kobold living in his house, by whose means he became a rich man. Among the forms which this Kobold sometimes took was that of a calf with fiery eyes, though more frequently he lay upon the hearth in the shape of an old cat. Sometimes he was found in the morning in the stove in the shape of a flame of fire; when the maid, suddenly frightened at the sight, would run to her mistress and tell her that there was a fiery monster in the grate, but by the time the mistress came he had vanished. This Kobold at length becoming too intimate with the good woman of the house, her husband one day caught him, packed him up in a basket, and had him carried away to such a distance that he could never find his way home again. The second passage describes the *Leuchtmannekens* (or little light-

men), as they are there called, as little spirits who
carry a light, and ofttimes so lead night wanderers out
of their road that it is long before they can find their
way again.   But that these spirits, (which are there
also described as the souls of unbaptized children who
cannot rest in their graves) are not always malicious,
but will sometimes do good service to those who know
how to propitiate them, is shown by the following
story :—

Close by Stulpe, and at the foot of the Gohn Mountain, these little light-men are often seen; and an old
man who had lived in that neighbourhood for many
years frequently saw them dancing merrily before
him as he returned home late at night from carousing
in the village.   If it was very dark, or a heavy fall
of snow had taken place, he would call out to one of
these little light-men, "Come, and light me home!"
This it would do instantly, going before him until he
had reached his dwelling-place, where it vanished.
Then he laid a halfpenny upon the sill of the door,
—and was sure to find it gone the next morning.
By that means, he secured the good offices of his
little attendants as he returned home from his next
merry-making.

But dismissing these *ignes fatui*, by referring the
reader desirous of knowing more of the Folk-Lore
which exists upon the subject of them to Mr. Jabez
Allies's interesting brochure " On the Ignis Fatuus,
or Will-o'-the-Wisp, and the Fairies"—and the scien-
tific inquirer as to the cause of the phenomenon to a
dissertation in the 51st livraison of the Revue Bri-
tannique entitled " Observations Physiques sur les
Feux-Follets," (an article which I have not had an
opportunity of consulting,)—let us turn our attention

to the trick which Puck played upon poor Bottom;
and, long as is the quotation, we must describe it in
Shakespeare's own inimitable language:—

" My mistress with a monster is in love.
  Near to her close and consecrated bower,
  While she was in her dull and sleeping hour,
  A crew of patches, rude mechanicals,
  That work for bread upon Athenian stalls,
  Were met together to rehearse a play,
  Intended for great Theseus' nuptial day.
    The shallowest thick-skin of that barren sort,
  Who Pyramus presented, in their sport
  Forsook his scene, and entered in a brake:
  When I did him at this advantage take,
  An ass's nowl I fixed on his head.
Anon, his Thisbe must be answered,
  And forth my mimic comes. When they him spy
  As wild geese that the creeping fowler eye,
  Or russet-pated choughs, many in sort,
Rising and cawing at the gun's report
  Sever themselves and madly sweep the sky;
So, at his sight, away his fellows fly:
  And, at our stamp, here o'er and o'er one falls;
  He murder cries, and help from Athens calls.
Their sense thus weak, lost with their fears, thus strong,
  Made senseless things begin to do them wrong:
  For briars and thorns at their apparel snatch;
Some sleeves; some hats; from yielders all things catch.
  I led them on in this distracted fear,
  And left sweet Pyramus translated there;
  When in that moment (so it came to pass)
  Titania waked and straightway loved an Ass."

Though " The Mad Pranks and Merry Jests of Robin Goodfellow," which Mr. Collier supposes Shakespeare to have been acquainted with, did not furnish
him with any authority for the ludicrous transformation which he makes Puck affect in the person of
honest " Nick Bottom," who had been selected to

play Pyramus, because "Pyramus is a sweetfaced
man,"—there can be little question that the possibility
of such transformations was in his day an article of
popular belief.

This may be inferred from the following passage
from Reginald Scot's "Discoveries of Witchcraft,"
book xiii., ch. 19: where he is speaking of certain
great matters that may be wrought by Art Magic:[*]

"As for example, if I affirm that with certain
charms and popish prayers I can set an horse or an
asses head upon a man's shoulders I shall not be believed; or if I do it I shall be thought a witch. And
yet, if L. Bap. Neap. experiments be true, it is no
difficult matter to make it seem so; and the charm of
a witch or papist joined with the experiment, will
also make the wonder seem to proceed thereof. The
words used in such case are uncertain, and to be re-
cited at the pleasure of the witch or cosener. But
the conclusion of this, cut off the head of a horse, or
an ass, (before they be dead, otherwise the vertue or
strength thereof will be the less effectual), and make
an earthen vessel of fit capacity to contain the same,
and let it be filled with the oyl and fat thereof, cover
it close, and dawb it over with lome; let it boyl over
a soft fire three days continually, that the flesh boyled
may run into oyl, so as the bare bones may be seen,
beat the hair into powder and mingle the same with
the oyl; and annoint the heads of the standers by,
and they shall seem to have horses or asses heads.
If beasts heads be anointed with the oyl made of a

---

[*] Although our quotation is from the edition dated in 1665,
it must be borne in mind that the book appeared as early
as 1584.

man's head, they shall seem to have men's faces, as divers authors soberly affirm."

This trick of Puck's may, however, have been suggested to Shakespeare by one that is related of the world-renowned Doctor Faustus. That Shakespeare knew of Faustus we see by his allusion to him in " The Merry Wives of Windsor," where Bardolph speaks of "three German devils, three Doctor Faustuses ":— and in the forty-third chapter of " The History of the Damnable Life and Deserved Death of Dr. John Faustus,"* which tells " how Dr. Faustus feasted his guests on Ash-Wednesday,"—we read, " The guests having sat, and well eat and drank, Dr. Faustus made that every one had an ass's head on, with great and long ears, so they fell to dancing, and to drive away the time until it was midnight, and then every one departed home, and as soon as they were out of the house, each one was in his natural shape, and so they ended and went to sleep." Now, although from the uncertainty which at present prevails as to when the English story-book was first printed it cannot be asserted that Shakespeare was acquainted with it, the probability is that he was so—or, at least, might have been. · In the first place, we know that the German Volksbuch, which corresponds with our English one, was printed at Frankfort in 1587 (and here let me remark that some of the German antiquaries have regarded the history of Faust as of English origin); and in the next place we have the fact that " The Second Report of Dr. John Faustus, containing his Appearances and the Deeds of Wagner," was pub-

---

* This is reprinted as well as " The Second Report " in the " Early Prose Romances," vol. iii.

lished in this country as early as 1594; from which
we may reasonably infer the existence of an earlier
edition of the tract before alluded to.

The readers of the beautiful German tales of Musäus doubtless remember his story of Rubezahl—or,
as the translator of the selection of them (said to be
no less a person than the late Mr. Beckford) which
appeared in 1791 under the title of "Popular Tales
of the Germans" anglicised his name, Number Nip.
They cannot have been otherwise than struck with
the resemblance between this tricksome spirit of the
Giant Mountains and our own Puck; but may probably have ascribed no small portion of this resemblance to the manner in which Musäus has told his
story. The resemblance is, however, very great;
and is perhaps still more so when read in the simple
legends in which Rubezahl figures, than in Musäus's
witty and spirited tale. These traditions were first
collected by Prætorius, in the middle of the seventeenth century, in a work which I have not had the
good fortune to have the opportunity of consulting.*
A selection of the merry tricks recorded by Prætorius
is inserted in Busching's Collection of Popular
Traditions, Tales, and Stories;† and with an extract
from one of these, which will serve to establish the resemblance between Puck and Rubezahl, and to show

---

* Under the title "Dæmonologia Rubinzalii Silesii," the
third edition of which was published at Leipsic in 1668.

† "Volks-Sagen, Marchen und Legenden," gesammelt von
J. G. Busching. The Rubezahl Legends form also the subject
of the following works :—I. "Die Wundersamen Mahrlein von
Berggeist Rubezahl," von Dr. Heinrich Doring, Leipzig, no
date. II. "Rubenzahl oder Volksagen im Reisenbirge," published in 1821 : and III. "Das Buch vom Rubezahl," &c., von
J. Lyser, Leipzig, 1834.

that the transformation which poor Bottom underwent was a common incident in works of popular fiction, we will conclude this chapter.—Rubezahl has been entertaining a party of guests in a deserted hostelry in which he had taken up his abode; and after having related the various proofs of his extraordinary powers which he had given, the story runs:—

And when they had been thus merry for some time, one among them said to Rubezahl, " Sir host, I pray you be so kind as to show us some pretty sportive jest." But Rubezahl said, " There is enough this time : this time you and the other lords have seen enough." All the lords agreed with Rubezahl, saying " The pastime would indeed be superfluous." But he who had spoken persevered, and begged so hard for one, as a sort of night-cap or sleeping draught, that Rubezahl at length said " It shall be so." In a trice this same guest had gotten on his shoulders an ox's head with great horns, just like the head of a real ox.

At this sight the rest of the company began to laugh at and mock him. This angered him, and he sought to reproach them for so doing, but when he tried to speak, he could only bellow for all the world as if he had been a living ox: and when he lifted a cup to his mouth and tried to drink out of it, he could not get a draught of wine, his lips were so much too large. At length Rubezahl's servant brought him some in a large vat, by which means he was enabled to get a hearty draught. Thus had the lords their sport with the ox; and well pleased were they with this merry jest.

In the meanwhile a rumour of what had happened reached the ears of this gentleman's wife; upon which she, with some of her companions, rode after her husband, and alighted at Rubezahl's dwelling. On entering she was informed that her husband had got an ox's head; and, when she found it was so, she addressed the foulest language to Rubezahl, for putting this shame upon her husband. Rubezahl spoke mildly to her in reply, telling her to hold her tongue. This, too, did the other guests; but in vain. Upon this Rubezahl conjured a cow's head, with horns complete, upon the poor woman's shoulders, at the sight of which the laughter increased; and when the poor woman tried to remonstrate, she only began to blare, and so did the ox likewise.

Merry indeed were all faces then, and right merrily wore they their caps: and in this spirit did the guests all go to sleep together, and snore the whole night through. And when they awoke early on the following morning, lo! there they all lay on an open heath. The occurrences of the preceding day seemed no more than a dream: yet some of them guessed shrewdly that this was a merry jest which had been put upon them by Rubezahl.

V.—THE NAMES OF SHAKESPEARE'S FAIRIES.

"Elves, list your names!"

THE several names by which the various members of the Elfin race are designated in the writings of Shakespeare mark as distinctly as any other of their characteristics the different elements out of which the beautiful system of our Fairy Mythology has been evolved: and to this subject it is that we now propose to direct the reader's attention.

That our *Fairies* derive that name, as well as many of their attributes, from the name *Fatæ*, by which the Parcæ of antiquity were sometimes designated, few who read Mr. Keightley's observations " On the Origin of the word Fairy "* will be inclined to doubt. And, although that gentleman has subsequently † ex-

---

* " Fairy Mythology," vol. i., p. 8 *et seq.*

† In his " Tales and Popular Fictions," p. 340, where he gives the following, as his perfect theory of the true origin of the word in question :—

" There can be no doubt that our word *Fairy* is the French *féerie,* which originally signified *illusion*, and is derived from *fée*. I therefore reject, with full convictions, all the Etymons (such as that from *Peri*) which go on the supposition of *Fairy* being the original name. The Italian *fata*, Provençal *fada*, French *faé, faée, fée*, are, beyond question, the words first used to designate the being whom we call *Fairy*. Of these words, I regard the Latin *fatum* as the root. In a coin of Diocletian the Destinies are, I know, named Fatæ, and this might seem to give a ready origin of the Italian and Provençal names, but there is so little resemblance between the *Parcæ* and the Fairies of romance, that I cannot adopt it. My opinion is, that, as from the Latin *gratus* came the Italian verb *aggradare*, and the French *agréer*, so from *fatum* came *affatare, fatare* Italian, and *faer, féer* French, signifying to enchant; and that *fato, fata, faé, faée, fée* are participles of these verbs. I believe there is not a single passage in the whole French romances in which these last words occur, in which they may not be taken participially : such are *les chevaliers faés, les dames faées*, and the continually recurring phrase *elle sembloit* (or *ressembloit*) *fée*. *La fée* is, therefore, *la femme fée*, and *une fée* is *une femme fée*. The Italian *fata* is, in the romantic poems, always employed as a substantive ; but it is well known that a number of substantives, in all languages, are in reality adjectives or participles, and in the " Pentamerone" *fata* and *fatata* are evidently employed as equivalents. I therefore regard *fata* as nothing more than *fatata*

pressed his disbelief of the identity of the Fatæ with
our modern Fairies, and confined himself to the view
which had originally been advanced by Tyrrwhitt,[*]
and subsequently by Price,[†]—namely, that the root
of our modern name of Fairy was to be found in the
Latin *fatum,*—it seems to us that further examination would have satisfied Mr. Keightley, as it has
satisfied Schreiber[‡] and Jacob Grimm,[§] that our
Fairies, as we have just stated, have derived that name,
as well as many of their attributes, from those spiritual beings whom Ausonius mentions as the *tria fata.*
To the Latin, at all events, we must look for the
origin of our word Fairy; and it is to be hoped we
shall hear no more of its being derived either from
the Persian Peri, or from that *fairness* of complexion
which is sometimes spoken of as one of the most
marked characteristics of the Fairy race.[‖]

The name *Elf* has not presented to the philologists
difficulties like those which they encountered in their
endeavours to discover the origin of the word *Fairy.*
In the latter case many of them were led by the
deceitful Will-o'-the-Wisp-like light of seeming and
specious etymons,

---

contracted after the usual rule of the Italian language, and
esteem *una fata* to signify merely *una donna fatata.*"

[*] In his note on the word *faerie,* in the Wife of Bath's Tale.
See Chaucer's "Canterbury Tales," vol. iv., p. 228 (ed. 1822).

[†] See his edition of Warton's "History of Poetry," vol. iv.,
p. 482, where he observes, that "the forms in which this word
(*fay* or *fée*) and its congeners exist in the romance dialects
seem to leave no doubt that the Latin *fatum* is its real source."

[‡] "Die Feen in Europa," s. l.

[§] "Deutsche Mythologie," s. 238.

[‖] See Brande's "Popular Antiquities" (ed. Ellis, 1841),
ii., 276.

" Over hill, over dale,'
Thorough bush, thorough briar,"

until they were left floundering in the very deepest
sloughs of etymological uncertainty. But the light
which has guided them to the origin of the word *Elf*
has been clear, distinct, and trustworthy; and all
have been enabled by its beams to discern that our
English name *Elf* is the same as the Anglo-Saxon
Alf, the old High German, and the middle High
German *Alp;* the old Norse *Alfr*, and the Gothic
Albs; and that corresponding with our English *Elf*,
in the plural *Elves*, we have the Swedish *Elf* in the
plural, *Elfvar* masculine and *Elfvor* feminine,—the
Danish *Elv* and *Elve* in the plural.

This word *Elf* has, however, undergone some
strange modifications. In Beowulf we read of—

" Eótenas and *Ylfe*
And Orcneas." *

" Eotens and Elves and Orcs;" and in Lazamon
again, as in the passage quoted from Sir F. Madden's
excellent edition in the first paper of this series,
we find them spoken of as *Alven*—

" Sone swa he com an eorthe   " So soon he came on earth
  Alven hine ivengen."   Elves received him."

Robert of Gloucester speaks of the *Elvene;* and
coming down to Shakespeare's own times, we find
Drayton in his exquisite piece of fairy poetry, " The
Nymphidia," using the word *aulf*—

" These, when a child haps to be got,
  Which after proves an idiot,
  When folks perceive it thriveth not,
  The fault therein to smother,

---

* See p. 9 of Mr. Kemble's edition.

> Some silly, doating, brainless calf,
> That understands things by the half,
> Says that the fairy left this *aulf*
> And took away the other."

From this *Aulf* the transition to *Ouphe*, another
of Shakespeare's fairy names, is very easy. This
latter designation of the elfin race occurs twice in
" The Merry Wives of Windsor." In the first place,
where Mrs. Page proposes—

> " Nan Page, my daughter, and my little son,
> And three or four more of their growth we'll dress
> Like urchins, *ouphes*, and fairies, green and white ;"

and in the second, where Mrs. Quickly, or rather
the Fairy Queen,* addresses this fairy band—for we
agree with Mr. Collier and Mr. Harness that the
speech should be spoken by her—

> " About, about ;
> Search Windsor Castle, elves, within and out :
> Strew good luck, *ouphes*, on every sacred room."

In a note on the former of these passages Steevens
boldly tells us that " *Ouphe* is the Teutonic word for
a fairy or goblin."† It may be ; but Grimm, who

---

* The following is Mr. Collier's note, and appears conclusive
upon the subject :—"At the suggestion of the Rev. Mr. Harness,
I have no difficulty in assigning this and other speeches to the
Fairy Queen or Anne Page so disguised : they are quite out of
character with Mrs. Quickly, to whom they have hitherto been
given. The prefix in the old copies is *Qu* and *Qui*, but it was
an easy error of the press, and much more probably so than that
such a part should have been intrusted to Mrs. Quickly.

† Mr. Collier has a far better note upon this passage in his
recent edition of Shakespeare, i., p. 255, "Ouphe" and *Elf* would
seem to have the same origin, the Teutonic *Alf*, a fairy or goblin.
It is variously spelt in our old writers, *Ofe*, *Auf*, and *Ophe*, as
well as *Ouphe*. The modern orthography is *Oaf*, and it generally means a dolt or blockhead.

probably knows quite as much of the Teutonic languages as did the Puck of Commentators himself, quotes no other authority for the word than Shakespeare. He sees in it only another form of the cognate *Elf;* and speaks of a corresponding form in the middle High German *Ulf,* in the plural *Ulve*—" von den *ulven* entbunden werden"—and proves the identity of this *Ulp* with *Alp,* and consequently with our English *Elf,* from a Swedish song published by Arwiddson, in his collection of Swedish ballads, in one version of which the elfin king is called " Herr *Elfver*," and in the second, " Herr *Ulfver.*" Hans Sachs, again, the worthy old shoemaker of Nuremburgh, used *ölp* " du *ölp* du dolp!" in the same sense as *Elf;* which again is nearly identical with *Alp* or *Olp,* a name given in Suffolk and many other parts of England to the bullfinch.*

Grimm, in his " Deutsche Mythologie," notices the connection which exists in many points between the elves of popular superstitions and bees; and in the same manner, that the name of the former should sometimes, as in the cases just referred to, be applied to the birds of the air, is easily understood when certain points of resemblance between them are taken into consideration. Thus, fairies and elves are often represented in flocks or troops, like birds; like birds

---

* See Major Moor's curious collection of Suffolk provincialisms, entitled " Suffolk Words and Phrases," under the words *Alp, Nope,* and *Olp.*

Alpe occurs too in the " Promptorium Parvulorum," where it is rendered " a byrde, *Ficedula*"—and Mr. Way, in his note, remarks *Ficedula,* a wodewale or an alpe, MED. GR. In Norfolk, the bullfinch is called Blood-olph, and the green Gros-beak, green Olf,· probably a corruption of Alpe, FORBY. Ray gives *Alp* as generally signifying the bullfinch.

too they fly away and vanish. A curious instance of the existence of this identity in popular opinion has lately been furnished me in a little Devonian legend: the result of an inquiry made of a country girl as to what she knew of the Pixies. She said she had never seen any; but that she had often heard of them,—and how they would *fly* into the houses at night, and make use of them. That they were often heard laughing and moving the furniture about; but that they always made the house very tidy before they went away, and always left a piece of silver at the bottom of a water jug. She added, that these Pixies often amused themselves by misleading people; and that she once " knew a man, who one night could not find his way out of one of his own fields, all he could do, until he recollected to *turn his coat;* and the moment he did so he heard the Pixies all *fly away up into the trees,* and there they sate and laughed—oh! how they did laugh!—but the man then soon found his way out of the field." Before concluding our notice of this word *ouphe,* we may remark that, in addition to the instances of Shakespeare's use of it which we have already quoted, it has been proposed to amend two other passages by its introduction. The first is in the " Comedy of Errors," where Theobald suggested, and very plausibly, that we should read,

" We talk with goblins, *ouphes,* and elvish sprites,"

instead of

" We talk with goblins, *owls,* and elvish sprites."

The second is in " The Merry Wives of Windsor," where Warburton proposed to amend that obscure passage—

"You orphan heirs of fixed destiny,"

by reading,

"You *ouphen* heirs of fixed destiny;"—

with what propriety, we shall find a better opportunity for discussing.

Urchin, another name applied by Shakespeare to the fairies, has served to vex the commentators, and this because it is an old name for a hedgehog. Thus, we find Steevens interpreting the first passage in "The Tempest," in which it occurs—

> "*Urchins*
> Shall, for that vast of night that they may work,
> All exercise on thee."

"*Urchins, i. e.* hedgehogs"—adding, "*Urchins* are enumerated by Reginald Scot among other terrific beings." And again, "*Urchins* are, *perhaps,* here put for fairies." Milton in his "Masque" speaks of "*urchin* blasts;" and we still call any dwarfish child an *urchin.* The word occurs again in the next act. Malone, not altogether satisfied with Steevens's note, says—"In ' The Merry Wives of Windsor' we have *urchins,* ouphes, and fairies;" and a passage, to which Mr. Steevens alludes inclines me to think that *urchins* here signify beings of the fairy kind—

> "His spirits hear me,
> And I need must curse; but they'll nor *pinch,*
> Fright me with *urchin-shows,* pitch me i' the mire,
> Nor lead me, like a fire-brand in the dark,
> Out of my way, unless he bids them."

How Steevens and Malone could read this latter passage, which forms so admirable an illustration of the manner in which the *urchins* were, for the vast of night that they might work, to exercise on Caliban,—and remembering as they did the combination of " urchins, ouphes, and fairies " in " The Merry Wives of Windsor," could yet doubt that *urchin* was used by Shakespeare as synonymous with elf and fairy, is most extraordinary. Lest, however, any of my readers should share that doubt, I subjoin in a note*

---

* " But certainly some one knave in a white sheet hath cosened and abused many thousands that way ; specially when Robin Goodfellow kept such a coil in the countrey ; but you shall understand that these bugs specially are spyed and feared of sick folk, children, women, and cowards, which, through weakness of mind and body, are shaken with vain dreams and continual fear. The Scythians, being a stout and warlike nation (as divers writers report), never see any vain sights or spirits. It is a common saying, ' A Lyon feareth no Bugs.' But in our childhood, our mothers' maids have so terrified us with an ugly Devil having horns on his head, fire in his mouth, and a tail in his breech, eyes like a bason, fangs like a dog, claws like a bear, a skin like a niger, and a voice roaring like a lyon, whereby we start and are afraid when we hear one cry Bough : and they have so frayed us with Bul-beggars, Spirits, Witches, *Urchens*, Elves, Hags, Faëries, Satyrs, Pans, Faunes, Sylens, Kit-with-the-Canstick, Tritons, Centaures, Dwarfes, Gyants, Imps, Calcars, Conjurors, Nymphes, Changelings, Incubus, Robin Goodfellow, the Spoorn, the Mare, the Man-in-the-Oak, the Hell-wain, the Firedrake, the Puckle, Tom-thombe, Hobgoblin, Tomtumbler, Boneless, and such other Bugs, that we are afraid of our shadows : insomuch that some never fear the Devil, but in a dark night ; and then a polled sheep is a perilous beast, and many times is taken for our fathers' soul, specially in a churchyard, where a. right hardy man heretofore scant durst passe by night but his hair would stand upright. For right grave writers report, that spirits most often and specially take the shape of Women, appearing to monks, &c., and of Beasts, Dogs, Swine, Horses, Goats, Cats, Hares ; of Fowles, as Crowes, Night Owles, and Shreeke Owles : but they delight most in the likeness of Snakes and Dragons. Well, thanks be to God, this wretched and cowardly infidelity, since the preaching of the Gospel, is in part forgotten : and

the passage from Reginald Scot, to which Steevens alluded,—and which should certainly have satisfied him that Shakespeare did *not* use the word *urchin* in the sense of hedgehog. I furnish them, too, with the following passage from Rowland,* in which urchins and elves are as closely identified as by Shakespeare—

> " In old wives daies, that in old time did live,
> (To whose odde tales much credit men did give)
> Great store of goblins, fairies, bugs, nightmares,
> *Urchins* and elves to many a house repaires."

And, lastly, I quote from my lamented friend, the late Mr. Douce's admirable "Illustrations of Shakespeare and of Ancient Manners," (vol. i., p. 11), " The Urchins' Dance," copied by him from a rare old collection of songs set to music by John Bennett, Edward Piers or Peirce, and Thomas Ravenscroft, composers in the time of Shakespeare, and entitled " Hunting, Hawking, Dauncing, Drinking, Enamoring," 4to., no date, which contains also the Elves' dance and the Fairies' dance—

> " *The Urchins' Dance.*
>
> By the moone we sport and play,
> With the night begins our day;
> As we friske the dew doth fall,
> Trip it little *urchins* all,
> Lightly as the little bee,

---

doubtless the rest of those illusions will in short time (by God's grace) be detected and vanish away." I have given this curious passage from the 15th chapter of the 7th book of Scot's " Discoverie "—first, because it is a curious illustration of the Folk-Lore of Shakespeare's time; secondly, in the hope that my readers will favour me with any allusions to the Spoorn, Calcars, the Man-in-the-Oak, Tom Tumbler, Boneless, &c., which they may meet with.

* " More Knaves yet. The Knaves of Spades and Diamonds," p. 114, of the edition of " The Four Knaves," edited by Mr. Rimbault for the Percy Society.

Two by two, and three by three,
And about goe wee, goe wee."

In the note from which this extract is taken, Mr. Douce, after remarking that " Mr. Steevens has observed that the *primitive* sense of *urchin* is a hedgehog, whence it came," says he, " to signify anything dwarfish," proceeds to remark, " There is, however, good reason for supposing it of Celtic origin. *Erch* in Welch is *terrible,* and *urzen* a superior intelligence. In the Bas-Breton language *urcha* signifies *to howl.*" *Urthin-wadd Elgin,* says Scot, in his " Discoverie of Witchcraft," (p. 224, ed. 1665,) " was a spirit in the days of King Solomon, came over with Julius Cæsar, and remained many hundred years in Wales, where he got the above name."

In confirmation of the accuracy of Mr. Douce's views as to the Celtic origin of the word *urchin* when used to designate a fairy, we may call attention to the *urisks* or Highland fairies, mentioned in Graham's " Sketches of Perthshire."

We may add, too, that near Inverness is a remarkable oblong mound, the name of which illustrates the present subject. It is called *Tom-na-Heurich,* or the Hill of the Fairies : and when we visited it in 1839 we were gravely told that it was once the dwelling-place of the fairies; and it seemed extremely doubtful whether our informant did not believe that they were still seen to issue from it occasionally.

May not the spirit *Ly Erg,* mentioned by Dalyell, in his " *Darker Superstitions of Scotland,*" be also connected with the subject of our present inquiry ? He is described as appearing with " a red hand in the habit of a souldier, and challenges men to fight with him ; as lately as 1669 he fought with three men, who died immediately after."

VI.—OF PUCK'S SEVERAL NAMES.

" Those that Hobgoblin call you, and sweet Puck,
  You do their work, and they shall have good luck."

HERE is, as has been already observed, much significance in the fact, that Shakespeare has bestowed upon

" That shrewd and knavish sprite
Called Robin Goodfellow"

the expressive name of Puck; and has thus distinguished Oberon's "trusty spirit" by no fanciful or imaginary epithet, but by a name which was in this country in Shakespeare's days a generic name applied to the whole race of Fairy :—as it still appears to be in certain districts of Worcestershire ;* and, as our extracts from Kohl's " Travels" have shown, it is still in Friesland also.

This name *Puck*—of which the earliest instance that occurs to us is in " Piers Ploughman," where it is used to signify the Devil—is perhaps the most remarkable of all the various designations by which the Fairy race have been distinguished, for, like that race, it seems to comprise within itself distinct traces of both Celtic and Teutonic elements.

---

* See Mr. J. Allies " On the Ignis Fatuus," p. 7; where we are told—" The peasantry in Alfrich, and those parts, say that they are sometimes what they call ' Poake ledden ;' that is, that they are occasionally waylaid in the night by a mischievous sprite whom they call Poake, who leads them into ditches, bogs, pools, and other such scrapes, and then sets up a loud laugh, and leaves them quite bewildered in the lurch."

Sir Francis Palgrave * was the first to call attention
to its etymological peculiarities, when remarking upon
the influence of language in embodying belief and
giving it tenacity:—" A curious exemplification of
this process," he remarks, " is afforded by the name
of Puck as applied to the Evil One, which also furnishes a striking proof of the steadiness with which
the meaning first annexed to a verbal sign adheres to
it through the modifications which it receives in language, whilst the mind retains the leading idea annexed
to the root with equal obstinacy. The gradual transition from delusion to sport and merriment, and from
sport and merriment to mischief, and from mischief
to terror, is very observable. *Pæccan* or *Pæccian*
(Anglo Saxon) signifies ' to deceive by false appearances, to delude, to impose upon.' In the cognate
Nether-Saxon, the verb *Picken* signifies to gambol;
and when inflected into *Pickeln* and *Paekeln*, to play
the fool. From the Anglo-Saxon root we have *Pack*
or *Patch*, the fool; whilst from *Pickeln* and *Paeckeln*
are derived *Pickle*, a mischievous boy; and the *Pickle-
härin* of the Germans, a merry-andrew, or zany, so
called, perhaps, from his hairy, or, perhaps, leafy vest-
ment. According to this analogy, Ben Jonson intro-
duces the devil *Puckhairy;* who probably appeared
in the shaggy garb which he is well known to have
worn in his character of Robin Hood, or Robin Goodfellow. *Pueke* and *Puck* are the sportive devils of
the Goths and Teutons. When used in a milder
sense, it becomes *Poike* (Sueo-Gothic), a boy, and
Piga (Anglo-Saxon), and *Pige* (Danish), a girl, from

* In his interesting paper on " The Popular Mythology of the
Middle Ages," in the 22nd volume of the "Quarterly Review."

their playfulness. *Pug* in Old English, and *Bogle* in Scottish, are equivalent to Puck; and some of our readers may not be aware that the monkey acquired his name of *Pug* from his malice. *Bwg*, in the British language, is a goblin; and *Bog*, the angry god of the Slavi, is still the same identical term. *Bucca* (Anglo-Saxon), a goat, and *Buck*, were so called from their skittish savage nature; the former being the favourite incarnation of Satan. In Βαϰϰεϰω we trace the mischievous mirth and wild inspiration caused by the delusion of wine: and we think that in *Peccare* we discern the agency of error and deceit."*

Price, the learned editor of Warton, followed up these Puckian etymologies, by observing† "that the *Puck* and the Scottish *Bogle* are the same as the German *Spuk* and the Danish *Spogelse*, without the sibilant aspiration. These words are general names for any kind of spirit, and correspond to the *Pouk* of ' Piers Ploughman.' In Danish *Spog* means a joke, trick, or prank; and hence the character of Robin Goodfellow. In Iceland *Puki* is regarded as an evil sprite; and in the language of that country ' *at pukra*' means both ' to make a murmuring noise ' and ' to steal clandestinely.' The names of these spirits seem to have originated in their boisterous temper. *Spuken* (German), to make a noise; *Spog* (Danish), obstrepe-

---

* The following is the author's note on this passage :—" The same root is possibly the origin of the *Bocket*, a *Larva* or *terriculamentum*, which schoolboys used to make by scooping out a turnip. A friendly antiquary suggests also that *Old Poker* or *Tom Poker*, who haunted the nursery in Horace Walpole's time, belongs to the same family. And we suppose him to have been the Sueo-Gothic *Tomte Pucke* or *House Puck*."

† In his preface to the edition of 1824. Vide vol. i., p. 31, ed. 1840.

rous mirth; *Pukke* (Danish), to boast, scold. The Germans use *Pochen* in the same figurative sense, though literally it means to strike, beat, and is the same with our *poke.* In Ditmarsch, the brownie, or domestic fairy, is called *Nitsche Puk.*"

To this goodly list of words supposed to be connected with Puck, Mr. Keightley added * the " Scottish *Pauky* and the Devonshire *Pixies.*"

To these we may add, from Dalyell,† the Scottish *Paichs,* an ancient diminutive race—to whose extraordinary strength the origin of Linlithgow Palace is ascribed; and from Grimm,—who looks upon *Puck* as connected with the Danish *Pog,* young; and so derived from the Finnish *Poica,* a son,—the Low German *Pook,* a little, under-sized person, and the North Friesian *Huspuke.*‡ Grimm, moreover, recognizes the identity of the Irish *Pooka,* and the Welsh *Pwcca* or *Bwcca,* with *Puck;* and these names clearly establish the proposition, that Puck, as a designation of the Fairy race, comprises within itself distinct traces of Celtic as well as of Teutonic elements.

To the former of these classes, too, belongs, in all probability, the Cornish *Piskey,* a name generally applied to the Fairies; but which is also, as we have been assured on most undoubted authority, a common appellation in the neighbourhood of Truro for moths; which are there believed by some to be fairies, by others, *departed souls.* As a consequence of this

---

* " Fairy Mythology," ii., p. 118, note.

† Dalyell's " Darker Superstitions of Scotland," p. 532. Dalyell notices, too, the *Pocclus* of the Samagitæ, mentioned by Lasicius, " De Dies Samagitarum," p. 54.

‡ " Deutsche Mythologie," s. 468.

latter belief, it is there thought that when moths are very numerous their appearance is an omen of a great mortality. The connection between this superstition and that article of the Folk-Lore of Greece which regarded the soul as a winged spirit, is not more remarkable than the identity which appears to exist between the names of the Grecian Ψυχὴ and the *Piskey* of Cornwall.

The *Puckrel*, an imp mentioned by Gifford, in his "Dialogue concerning Witches and Witchcraft,"* closes this somewhat extensive list of names which resemble one of those that were so pleasing to Oberon's Messenger as always to propitiate his favour and secure his friendly offices.

Let us now consider the other epithet which sounded so sweetly in his ears—namely, Hobgoblin.

The latter portion of this compound epithet is, of course, derived from the Greek κόβαλος, and the Latin *Cobalus*, through the Middle Latin *Gobelinus* and the French *Gobelin*. Grimm remarks that the character of this domestic spirit resembles in many points that of the Jester; and he refers to the German *Narrenkolbe* as corresponding with the English *Hobgoblin*, which he states to be the same as *Clowngoblin*.†

---

* See p. 9 of the Percy Society's reprint of the edition of 1603—"He showed him her in a glasse, and told him she had three or four impes, some call them *puckrels*," &c.

† This Grimm does on the authority of Nares; who states, however, that *Hob* was also used as a substitute for *Hobgoblin*, and quotes as his authority Beaumont and Fletcher's "Monsieur Thomas"—

"From Elves, *Hobs* and Fairies
That trouble our dairies,
From Fire-drakes and Fiends,
And such as the Devil sends,
Defend us, good Heaven!"

He afterwards refers to the practice of bestowing upon these spirits Christian names, in their diminutive forms, as a proof of the familiarity of intercourse which existed between mankind and this elfin race; and of which the English *Robin Goodfellow*, and the Danish *Nissen Goddreng* furnish us with striking instances. Now *Hob*, although very generally used to signify a clown or countryman, as in the old poem quoted by Steevens, in one of his notes on Coriolanus,

> "The country gnuffs, Hob, Dick, and Hick,"

is also the familiar or diminutive form of Robert and Robin, so that Hobgoblin is equivalent to Robin the Goblin, *i. e.* Robin Goodfellow. This is borne out by the passage in the "Nymphidia," in which, when describing Oberon's first encounter with his trusty messenger, Drayton says—

> "He meeteth Puck, which most men call
> Hob-goblin, and on him doth fall
>   With words from frenzy spoken,
> 'Hoh! Hoh!' quoth Hob, 'God save thy Grace!
> Who dressed thee in this piteous case?
> He thus that spoiled my sov'reign's face
>   I would his neck were broken;'"

for in this case Hob is clearly used as a proper name. And with reference to the present point, it may be remarked, that the Will-o'-the-Wisp, which, as we have seen, is one of the forms commonly assumed by Puck, is called in Worcestershire by the several names of "Hob-and-his-Lanthorn," "Hobany's Lanthorn," and "Hoberdy's Lanthorn."*

---

* See Mr. Allies's pamphlet "On the Ignis Fatuus," p. 3, where it is stated that in the neighbourhood of *Alfrich* (i. e.)

In another of the epithets—namely, that by which
the Fairy addresses Puck in the first scene in the
" Midsummer Night's Dream," in which the shrewd
and knavish sprite makes his appearance—

"Thou Lob of Spirits!"—

some of the commentators see, and very correctly, no
doubt, an allusion to the " lubber fiend " spoken of
by Milton. Dr. Johnson's observation that Lob,
Lubber, Looby, Lobcock, all denote both inactivity
of body and dulness of mind is in the present case
altogether misplaced. For here the name *Lob* is
doubtless a well-established fairy epithet: and the
passage quoted by Steevens from Beaumont and
Fletcher's " Knights of the Burning Pestle," confirms this:—" There is a pretty tale of a witch that
had the devil's mark about her, that had a giant to
be her son, that was called *Lob-lye-by-the-Fire*."
Grimm mentions a remarkable document, dated in
the year 1462, in which Bishop Gebhard, of Halber-
stadt, complains of the reverence paid to a spirit
called *den guden lubben,* the good *lubbe,* and to whom
bones of animals were offered on a mountain near
Schochwitz in the district of Mansfeld. " Not only,"
adds Grimm,* " have piles of such bones been discovered on the *Lup*-berge, but at the neighbouring
church of Müllersdorf there is an idol built into the
wall which is traditionally said to have been brought
there from the Lupberge, or Lubbe mountain."
Presuming *Lob* to be, as we believe it is, a decided

Elf-reich, or Fairy-land, a name sufficiently significant as a
proper locality for such traditions), where the Ignes fatui are
thus designated, the so-called fairy-rings are very abundant.
  * " Deutsche Mythologie," s. 492.

fairy epithet, it furnishes an explanation of a phrase
which has hitherto been a puzzle to the commentators—namely, Lob's Pound; under which heading
we read in Nares as follows:—" *To be laid in Lob's
Pound,* to be 'laid by the heels or clapped up in
jail' (*Old Canting Dictionary*); also, any close or
confined place; as in the following lines it means
' behind the arras : '—

> ' Who forced the gentleman, to save her credit,
> To marry her, and say he was the party
> Found in *Lob's Pound.'*
> > Massinger's *D. of Milan,* iii. 2.

" Who *Lob* was is as little known as the site of
Lipsbury Pinfold. In ' Hudibras ' this term is em-
ployed as a name for the stocks, into which the
Knight puts Crowdero—

> ' Crowdero, whom in irons bound,
> Thou basely threw'st into *Lob's Pound.'*
> > I. iii. 909.

Dr. Grey, in the notes, tells a ludicrous application
of it in the case of one *Lobb,* a dissenter minister."

But when we interpret *Lob* by Fairy, we can
easily understand the application of the name *Lob's
Pound* to those fairy rings, circlets, or dances, from
which those who had once entered them could not
extricate themselves; and of which Old Aubrey*
has left the following characteristic notice:—" In
the yeare 1633-4, soone after I had entered into my
grammar at the Latin schoole at Yatton Keynel, our
curate, Mr. Hart, was annoy'd one night by these

---

* Halliwell's " Illustrations of the Fairy Mythology of the
Midsummer Night's Dream," printed for the Shakespeare
Society, p. 235.

elves or fayries. Comming over the downes, it being neere darke, and approaching one of the faiery
dances, as the common people call them in these
parts, viz. the greene circles made by those sprites
on the grasse, he all at once sawe an innumerable
quantitie of pigmies, or very small people, dancing
rounde and rounde, and singing, and making all
maner of small odd noyses. He being very greatly
amaz'd, and yet not being able, as he sayes, to run
away from them, being, as he supposes, kept there
in a kinde of enchantment; they no sooner perceave
him, but they surround him on all sides, and what
betwixt feare and amazement, he fell down, scarcely
knowing what he did; and thereupon these little
creatures pinch'd him all over, and made a sort of
quick humming noyse all the time; but at length
they left him, and when the sun rose he found himself exactly in the midst of one of these faiery dances.
This relation I had from him myselfe, a few days after
he was so tormented; but when I and my bedfellow
Stump wente soon afterwards at night time to the
dances on the downes, we sawe none of the elves or
fairies. But indeede, it is saide, they seldom appeare
to any persons who go to seeke for them."

In conclusion, we would remark, as curiously illus-
trating the subject of the present paper, that in
" Piers Ploughman " we meet with " *Poukes pond-
fold:* "

> " Out of the *poukes pondfold*
> No maynprise may us fecche
> Till he come that I carpe of,
> Crist is his name."

Hell is here spoken of as the " Pouk or Devil's
Pound:" and certainly this expression goes far to

support our opinion that *Lob's Pound* was originally used in the same manner to express the fairy circlets from which those who once entered them could by no means escape.

VII.—QUEEN MAB.

"*Mercutio.* Oh, then I see Queen Mab has been with you.
Benvolio. Queen Mab! What's she?"—*Ed.* 1597.

THE whole Fairy Mythology of Shakespeare, varied and extensive as it is, does not present us with any subject so pregnant with curious speculation as is the exquisite description of the Fairy Queen which he has placed in the mouth of Mercutio, in reply to that question of Benvolio, "Queen Mab! what's she?"—which we agree with Mr. Hunter in thinking "ought by all means to be retained, as affording a just pretence for the long description of the practices and attributes of Queen Mab that follows:"[*]

"She is the fairies' midwife; and she comes
  In shape no bigger than an agate stone
  On the fore-finger of an alderman,
  Drawn with a team of little atomies
  Over men's noses as they lie asleep:
  Her waggon-spokes made of long spinners' legs;
  The cover, of the wings of grasshoppers;
  The traces, of the smallest spider's web;
  The collars, of the moonshine's watery beams;
  Her whip, of cricket's bone; the lash, of film:
  Her waggoner, a small grey-coated gnat
  Not half so big as a round little worm
  Prick'd from the lazy finger of a maid.

---

[*] "New Illustrations of the Life, Studies and Writings of Shakespeare," ii. 135.

Her chariot is an empty hazel nut,
Made by the joiner squirrel or old grub,
Time out of mind the fairies' coachmakers.
And in this state she gallops night by night
Through lovers' brains, and then they dream of love—
On courtiers' knees, that dream on court'sies straight—
O'er lawyers' fingers, who straight dream on fees—
O'er ladies' lips, who straight on kisses dream ;
Which oft the angry Mab with blisters plagues
Because their breaths with sweetmeats tainted are.
Sometime she gallops o'er a courtier's nose,
And then dreams he of smelling out a suit ;
And sometime comes she with a tithe-pig's tail,
Tickling a parson's nose as 'a lies asleep,
Then he dreams of another benefice.
Sometime she driveth o'er a soldier's neck,
And then dreams he of cutting foreign throats,
Of breaches, ambuscadoes, Spanish blades,
Of healths five fathom deep ; and then anon
Drums in his ear, at which he starts and wakes ;
And, being thus frighted, swears a prayer or two,
And sleeps again.   This is that very Mab,
That plats the manes of horses in the night ;
And bakes the elf-locks in foul sluttish hairs,
Which, once untangled, much misfortune bodes.
This is the hag, when maids lie on their backs
That presses them, and learns them first to bear,
Making them women of good carriage.
This, this is she."

In this admirable outpouring of Shakespeare's abundant fancy we see the Fairy Queen—not, as in the " Midsummer Night's Dream," graced with a name borrowed from Shakespeare's classical recollections, and in that name, as in many of her attributes, bearing strong marks of her affinity to

" Modest Dian, circled with her nymphs,"

but she is here presented to us under a totally different aspect—under a name which, although it has hitherto passed without notice from the commentators, calls for much examination; and invested with properties which identify her with the Night Hag of popular superstition.   This fact furnishes us with another proof how intricately the many-coloured web of that superstition is interwoven.   When considering the name of Puck, we have seen how closely that epithet identifies the Fairies with the race of Fallen Angels; and in this beautiful passage from " Romeo and Juliet," we find the Fairy Queen invested with the attributes of one of the most repulsive and the most dreaded of all the mysterious creations which the busy imagination of uninstructed man has ever called into existence.

And that this connection between the powers of the elfin race and the dreaded visitations of the Nightmare arises from no confusion in the mind of Shakespeare, is evident from the fact, that his great predecessor Chaucer has shown us, in a well-known passage of " The Wife of Bath's Tale," that such connection belonged to the Folk-Lore of his times:

> " In olde dayes of the Kyng Arthour,
> Of which that Britouns speken great honour,
> Al was this lond fulfilled of fayrie :
> The elf-queen, with hir jolie compaigne,
> Daunced ful oft in many a grene mede.
> This was the old oppynyoun as I rede ;
> I speke of many hundrid yer ago ;
> But now can no man see noon elves mo.
> For now the grete charite and prayeres
> Of lymytours and other holy freres,
> That sechen every lond and every streem,
> As thik as motis in the sonne-beem,
> Blessynge halles, chambres, kichenes and boures,
> Citees and burghes, castels and hihe toures,
> Thropes and bernes, shepnes and dayeries,

That maketh that ther ben no fayeries.
For ther as wont was to walken an elf,
Ther walkith noon but the lymytour himself,
In undermeles and in morwenynges
And saith his matyns and his holy thinges
As he goth in his lymytacion.
Wommen may now go saufly up and doun ;
In every bussch, and under every tre,
Ther is non other incubus but he,
And he ne wol doon hem no dishonour." •

And in " The Miller's Tale," in which Chaucer has
introduced an old charm against the Nightmare, we
have the identity between the

> " Fairies and the tempters of the night"

as clearly marked as it is in the prayer of Imogen.
The carpenter is speaking to Nicholas, who is apparently in a trance, or under the influence of an evil
spirit :—

" This Nicholas sat stille as any stoon,
And ever he gapyd up-ward to the eyr.
This carpenter wende he were in despeir,
And hent him by the schuldres mightily,
And schook him harde, and cryed spitously,
' What, Nicholas ? what how man, loke adoun :
Awake and thynk on Christes passioun ;
I crowche the from elves, and from wightes.'
Therwith the night-spel seyde he anon rightes
On the foure halves of the hous aboute,
And on the threisshfold of the dore withoute.
' Lord Jhesu Crist, and seynte Benedight,
Blesse this hous from every wikkede wight,
Fro nightes verray,† the white Paternoster ;
Wher wonestow now, seynte Petres soster.' "

• See vol. i., pp. 138 and 139, of " The :Canterbury Tales
of Geoffrey Chaucer," a New Text, with Illustrative Notes,
edited by Thomas Wright, Esq., M.A., for the Percy Society.

† Mr. Wright, from whose edition (vol. i., p. 139) we have

But the most striking proof of this identity is to be found in Drayton's "Nymphidia,"—where, after a description of the palace of the fairy sovereigns, we read:—

> " Hence Oberon him sport to make,
> (Their rest when weary mortals take
> And none but only fairies wake),
>   Descendeth for his pleasure :
> And Mab, his merry queen, by night
> Bestrides young folks that lie upright,
> (*In elder times the Mare that hight*),
>   Which plagues them beyond measure."

The propriety with which Shakespeare has invested Queen Mab with the attributes of the Nightmare is confirmed by an examination of the popular belief upon the subject as it now exists among the Continental nations. Among some of these, it is designated the *Alp*,—thereby pointing most distinctly to its elfin nature. Thus, in Altmark, as we read in Kuhn's "Markische Legenden," the *Alb* is believed to seat himself on the body of a sleeping person, and so cause horrible dreams. The best way of relieving a person so tormented is to call him by his Christian name. The *Mahre*, who is said to resemble the Alb in her nature, is represented as assuming the form of a beautiful female spirit, who

---

made this quotation, observes, in a note, "*Verray* is the reading of the MSS. I have consulted. Tyrwhitt reads *mare*, which is perhaps right." Tyrwhitt tells us (vol. iv., p. 197), "the charm is so lamely represented in all the MSS., that I have left it as I found it in the common editions." Speght gives us the couplet—
> " Fro the night's mare the wite Paternoster
>   Wher wonnest thou saint Peter's suster ;"
and is followed by Urry almost to a letter.

can be seized by closing all means of escape from the chamber; and who certainly cannot glide away if laid hold of by a person wearing gloves:—and tradition speaks of persons being married for years to such a spirit, or Mahre,—who has afterwards suddenly disappeared from them.

I do not propose to trespass upon the patience of the reader by producing one tithe of the legends connected with the Nightmare which are to be found in the traditionary stores of Germany and Flanders, Denmark and Norway,—or in the dissertations by the many authors, lay and clerical, who have made witchcraft and demonology the subject of their speculations. But with the view of satisfying him how faithfully Shakespeare has represented the Folk-Lore of his own time when he identified the Nightmare with the Queen of the Fairies—which fairies or elves, it must be borne in mind, were sometimes most malignant in their nature and most inimical to man— I must call his attention to a German legend of the Alp, as it is preserved in the " Deutsche Sagen"* of the Brothers Grimm.

" It is in· vain to close both doors and windows carefully against the Alps : they can creep in at the smallest cranny, and have an especial delight in seeking out such. The noise which they make in the walls when so employed is often heard in the stillness of night. If, when they have entered the room, the hole by which they gained admittance is suddenly stopped up, they cannot away, although

---

* Band, I. s. 130. Grimm quotes, as the authority for this description of the Alp, oral tradition, Prætorius " Weltbeschreibung" (I. 1–40, II. 160–162), and Brauner's " Curiositaten," 126–137.

both doors and windows should be thrown open. Then is the time to extort from them a promise never more to disturb that place. On such occasions they have frequently been known to complain most grievously that they may have left their children at home, who must perish if they are not set free.

" The Trud or Alp often travels a great distance on these nocturnal trips. Once upon a time some shepherds who were tending their flocks in the middle of the night, in some pastures on the banks of a river, saw an Alp come thither, jump into a boat, cast it off from the shore, and ferry himself across by means of a staff which he brought with him. He then moored the boat on the other side, and went on his way. After a time, he returned and ferried himself over as before. The shepherds, after they had watched for several nights and seen the same thing repeated, took measures to remove the boat as soon as he had crossed the river. When the Alp returned he began to make great lamentations, and threatened the shepherds · that they should never have any peace until they restored his boat;—which at last they were obliged to do.

" A man once laid a hackel or flax comb upon his stomach for the purpose of keeping off the Alp; but the Alp turned it round, and so drove the points of it into the man's flesh. A better preventative is, however, to turn the shoes before the bed, so that the heels are next to the bedstead. When a man is oppressed by the Alp, if he can only grasp his thumb in his hand, the Alp must vanish. At night the Alp often rides the horses, so that in the morning they are found quite tired out. But he can be kept away by horse-heads. Whoever before he goes to sleep

does not move his stool to another place, will that
night be ridden by the Mahre. They delight in giving
people elf-locks (*weichel-zopfe*) by sucking and entangling their hair. * * If any person oppressed by
the Alp says,.

Trud komm Morgen	Trud come to-morrow,
So will ich borgen	So shalt thou borrow,

it immediately vanishes, and comes next morning in
the form of a man to borrow something. Or if any
body calls after the Alp ' Come to-morrow and drink
with me !' the person who sent the Alp is compelled
to come.

" According to Prætoriüs, the eyebrows of the Alp
meet together in a straight line; others say that
people whose eyebrows meet together on the fore-
head have the power, by a mere exercise of the
thoughts, to send the Alp to any one towards whom
thèy feel hate or anger. The Alp then issues from
their eyes, assumes the form of a small white butter-
fly, and settles upon the other party when sleeping."

It can scarcely be necessary to call the reader's
attention to the points in the foregoing quotation,
which will serve to confirm the view which it is the
object of the present paper to establish—namely, the
identity of the Fairy Queen Mab and the Incubus
Ephialtes, or Nightmare. We think the facts in the
legend which Grimm has preserved, that the Hag
bears the name of *Alp*—which is equivalent to *Elf*,
and consequently to Fairy—and is, like the Elfin
Queen Mab, represented as

"Platting the manes of horses in the night,"
and
"Baking the elf-locks in foul sluttish hairs,"

are quite sufficient to make our readers identify the two,—and, whether we point to Alp or Mab, exclaim with Mercutio,

> " This, this is she."

Of the name of Mab, and of the attributes with which Shakespeare, echoing the popular voice, has invested her, we shall speak hereafter.

VIII.—QUEEN MAB: HER NAME AND ATTRIBUTES.

> " This is that very Mab
> That plats the manes of horses in the night,
> And bakes the elf-locks in foul sluttish hairs,
> Which once untangled, much misfortune bodes.
> This is the hag when maids lie on their backs
> Which presses them.—This, this is she."

NE of the most striking of the elfin characteristics set forth in the foregoing passage, and one by which Mab the Fairy Queen, and the Alp or Nightmare are equally distinguished—namely, that of

> " Baking the elf-locks in foul sluttish hairs,"—

is one which they share in common not only with *Aitwaras*, the Incubus of Lithuanian superstition, but also with Frau Holle, who plays so distinguished a part in the popular mythology of the Germans. Frau Holle is not only represented as being rendered still more hideous by having her own long hair elfed into knots, but as also so entangling the locks of others: and hence " he has been with Mother Holle " is an expression commonly applied to any person whose hair is particularly rough, matted and untidy. Frau Holle, or Hulda, as she is sometimes designated, it may be remarked, resembles, too, the sovereign of the fairy race in many other particulars besides her propensity to steal unbaptized children. She is sometimes represented as fair and young— sometimes as altogether the reverse; and oftentimes she appears not alone, but as the head or queen of a race of spirits who are called after her *Huldrefolk.*[*] Like Woden, again, Frau Holle takes her nightly course through the air; and, like that well-known mythic hero, forms a portion of the wild host which used formerly to terrify by their unearthly cries the belated peasantry of Germany.

But there was another personage who, according to the popular voice, was accustomed to take part in these nocturnal flights—these *chasses fantastiques,* as they are designated in France—whose name has never, I believe, been brought under the notice of the English reader, except by the late Mr. Douce, (in his long, curious, and interesting note upon Shakespeare's introduction of Hecate among modern witches),[†]—although that name is very possibly connected with that of our own Mab,—whom she unquestionably so far resembles, that one of her peculiarities is her

" Platting the manes of horses in the night."

I allude to *Dame Abunde* or *Habunde;* whom Mr. Douce describes as " having been the *genuine queen*

---

[*] See Grimm's "Deutsche Mythologie," s. 249.

[†] " Illustrations of Shakespeare and of Ancient Manners," vol. i., p. 382, *et seq.*

of fairies, and of a most innocuous and benevolent
disposition, bestowing happiness and *abundance* on
all her votaries.   In support of this latter statement
he quotes an ancient fabliau by Haisau, which has
never been entirely printed, in which she is thus introduced—

> " Ceste richesse nus abonde
> Nos lavons de par Dame Avonde,"—

and adds, " She is also mentioned in the works of
William Auvergne, Bishop of Paris in the fourteenth
century, as a spirit enriching the houses that she
visited."

Grimm, in his elaborate notice of Dame Abunde,
furnishes us with the passage from William of Auvergne, to which Mr. Douce alludes when speaking
of that important personage; and also with one
which, from its connection with another superstition
connected with the present inquiry, is no less interesting—namely, that in which the worthy Bishop of
Paris speaks of certain hags, or malicious spirits, who
were sometimes seen in stables with waxen lights,
from which they suffered drops to fall on the necks
and manes of the horses—and of the manes of the
latter being carefully plaited " *comæ ipsorum diligenter
tricatæ.*" *

---

* This passage is sufficiently curious to be quoted at length.
It is found at p. 1066, of vol. i. of the edition of the Bishop's
collected works, published at Paris in 1674.—" Sunt et aliæ
ludificationes malignorum spirituum, quas faciunt interdum in
nemoribus et locis amœnis et frondosis arboribus, ubi apparent
in similitudine *puellarum* aut matronarum ornatu muliebri et
candido, interdum etiam in stabulis, cum luminaribus cereis, ex
quibus apparent distillationes in comis et collis equorum, et

This superstition appears to have been very widely circulated; and Mr. Douce, in his observations upon it, mentions a very uncommon old print by Hans Burgmair relating to it,—in which a witch is represented as entering the stable with a lighted torch, and previously to the operation of entangling the horse's mane practising her enchantments on the groom who is lying asleep on his back, and apparently under the influence of the Nightmare.

Of the connection which would seem to be established by means of community of attribute between Queen Mab and those female deities which, as *Dominæ Nocturnæ, Bonæ Mulieres,* or *Bonnes Dames,* are so frequently mentioned by the mediæval writers, and formed a peculiar hierarchy under their queen who, whether she be called Diana, Bensozia, Berchta, Befania, Abundia, Folla, Hulda, Frau Gaude, Herka, Hruoda, Ostara, Ostavia, Herodias, or Astarte, is, according to Schreiber,[*] no other than the Queen of Heaven herself—Regina Cœli, Virgo Cœlestis, Bona Dea Sanctissima Cœlestis, Invicta Cœlestis Urania, &c.,—we have not here, and at this time, an opportunity of treating in the manner which the subject demands.

We will, therefore, proceed to consider briefly the name which Shakespeare has in " Romeo and Juliet" bestowed upon the sovereign of the fairy race— namely, Queen Mab.

The reader to whom the writings of Shakespeare,

---

comæ ipsorum diligenter tricatæ, et audies eos, qui talia se vidisse fatentur, dicentes veram ceream esse, quæ de luminaribus hujusmodi stillaverat."

[*] Schreiber, " Die Heren und Feen," s. 107.

Drayton, Herrick, the Duchess of Newcastle, and others have made the name of Queen Mab as familiar as the veriest household word, will probably be surprised to learn that no earlier instance of Mab being used as the designation of the Fairy Queen has hitherto been discovered than that of Shakespeare in his " Romeo and Juliet." He will probably be almost as much surprised when he is told that none of the commentators, wide as is their reading, extensive as have been their labours, appear to have sought to ascertain either what authority Shakespeare had for so designating the fairies' midwife, or what is the meaning of the designation which he in his " Romeo and Juliet " thought fit to bestow upon her.   This is the more extraordinary since none can doubt that Mab is a genuine name,—and not like those which Drayton, who designates the Fairy Queen by it, has bestowed upon the members of her fairy court—

> " Hop and Mop and Dyp so clear,
>   Pip and Trip and Skip that were
> To Mab, their sovereign ever dear, ,
>   Her special maids of honour ;
> Fib and Tib and Pinck and Pin,
> Tick and Quick and Jil and Jin,
> Tit and Nit and Wap and Win,
>   The train that wait upon her "—

or Shakespeare's own Peas-blossom, Cobweb, and Mustard-seed,—names created for the nonce, and begotten of the poet's fancy.   But though it is easy to decide—what is unquestionably the case—that Shakespeare learned that Mab was the name of the Fairy Queen from the Folk-Lore of his own time,— for the name of Mab appears to have been at one time current in Warwickshire, where, as we learn from a note of Sir Henry Ellis, in his edition of

Brand, " Mab-led, pronounced Mob-led, signifies led astray by a Will-o'-the-Wisp,"*—what is the meaning of that name Mab, and why it was originally applied to the sovereign of fairy land, are questions far more difficult of solution.

Looking to the general character given of *Dame Abunde*, or *Habunde*—the story of her visiting houses at night, and partaking of the wine and good things purposely left out for her, as, we learn from William d'Auvergne† the practice was,—and looking also to her nightly trips, to which Meon also alludes in his " Roman de la Rose," where he says—

> " Que les cinc sens ainsinc deçoit
> Par les fantosmes, qu'il reçoit,
> Dont maintes gens par lor folie
> Cuident estre par nuit estries
> Errans aveques *Dame Habonde*," &c.

I at one time felt inclined to answer in the affirmative Mr. Keightley's question,‡ Is Mab a contrac-

---

* " Popular Antiquities," vol. iii., p. 218 (ed. 1841).

† The following is the good Bishop's account, which we extract the rather since we believe it has never hitherto been laid before the English reader. In the original it follows the passage given in a former note. " De illis vero substantiis, quæ apparent in domibus, quas *dominas nocturnas*, et *principem* earum vocant *dominam Abundiam*, pro eo quod domibus, quas frequentant, abundantiam bonorum temporalium præstare putantur, non aliter tibi sentiendum est, quam quemadmodum de illis audivisti. Quapropter eo usque invaluit stultitia hominum et insania vetularum, ut vasa vini et receptacula ciborum disco operta relinquant, et omnino nec obstruant neque claudant eis noctibus, quibus ad domos suos eas credant adventuras, ea de causa videlicet, ut cibos et potus quasi paratos inveniant et eos absque difficultate apparitionis pro beneplacito sumant."— GRIMM, " Deutsche Mythologie," s. 264.

‡ " Fairy Mythology," vol. ii., p. 135. The following is, I

tion of Habundia, who, Heywood tells us, ruled over the fairies?—more especially since it appeared that Dame Abonde might possibly have been contracted into Dame Ab, and thence into Mab. Another derivation may be from *Mabel* (of which *Mab* is, I believe, a common abbreviation); and respecting which Camden in his "Remains" says, "Some will have it to be a contraction of the Italians from *Mabella*, that is, my fair daughter or maid. But whereas it is written in deeds *Amabilia* and *Mabilia*, I think it cometh from *Amabilis*, that is, loveable or lovely."

Further consideration, has, however, satisfied me that the origin of this name Mab is to be found in the Celtic. Beaufort, in his "Antient Topography of Ireland," mentions *Mabh* as the chief of the Irish fairies. When speaking of the Fiodha Rhehe, he says—"*Fiodha Rhehe* pronounced Fairy, that is, sylvan divinities, from *Fiodha* woods, and *Rhehe*. The *Fiodha Rhehe*, in the ancient Celtic Mythology, were subordinate genii who presided over the vegetable productions of nature and the animals of the forest. They were the satyrs and elves of the Greeks and Romans; the chief of whom was Pan or Pallas, called by the ancient Irish, Mogh, Magh, or *Mabh.* The notion of fairies so prevalent amongst the country people at this day is the remains of this heathen superstition."[*] Afterwards, which is more to our pre-

---

presume, the passage from Heywood's "Hierarchie of the Blessed Angells," lib. 8, p. 507, to which Mr. Keightley alludes—
  "One kinde of these th' Italians *Fatæ* name;
  Feé, the French; we, Sybils; and the same
  Others, White Nymphs; and those that have them seen;
  Night-Ladies, some, of which *Habundia* Queene."
  [*] No. xi. in vol. iii. of Vallancey's "Collectanea de Rebus Hibernicis." See p. 350.

sent purpose, Beaufort clearly identifies *Mabh* with Diana. He is speaking of the chief of the genii, who in the old Irish and Celtic Mythology presided over the various productions of nature, and of the names which this divinity received according to the different departments it was supposed to occupy; and he goes on to say, " when presiding over the forests and chief of the *Fiodh Rhehe*" (which, as we have already seen, were fairies, corresponding with the satyrs and elves of the Greeks and Romans), " it was denominated *Mabh* by the Irish, by the Greeks *Diana*, and by the Romans *Pan*."

Before meeting with the foregoing passages, which are certainly curiously illustrative of the present inquiry, I had satisfied myself of the Celtic origin of the name of Mab,—but upon very different grounds; for I saw in this designation a distinct allusion to the diminutive form of the elfin sovereign. *Mab*, both in Welsh and in the kindred dialects of Brittany, signifies a child or infant; and my readers will, I am sure, agree with me that it would be difficult to find any epithet more befitting one who

> " Comes
> In shape no bigger than an agate stone
> On the forefinger of an alderman ;"

that dwarf-like sovereign whose tiny subjects are employed—

> " Some to kill cankers in the musk rose-buds,
> Some war with rear mice for their leathern wings
> To make her small elves coats ;"—

and who when frighted with the domestic squabbles of their rulers,

> " for fear
> Creep into acorn cups and hide them there."

Here let me sing, with Bishop Corbet,

" Farewell Rewards and Fairies ! "

and for awhile bring to a close so much of the illustrations of the Folk-Lore of Shakespeare as relates
to the Fairy Mythology of England.   There are
many points connected with it still untouched ; but
the consideration of which it has seemed good to
defer to some more convenient opportunity.   Frag-
mentary, however, as have been my notices of it,
I trust they have shown the varied origin of that
beautiful portion of our Popular Mythology of which
Shakespeare has made such admirable and effective
use, and have convinced my readers that, however
gorgeous the colouring, however skilful the grouping,
the pictures of the elfin race which Shakespeare has
left us have the additional charm of being truthful
copies of the originals from which he drew, and
which he found enshrined in the hearts and memories
of his contemporaries.

IX.—The Owl was a Baker's Daughter.

" *Ophelia.* Well ! God 'ield you ! They say, the Owl was a
baker's daughter.   Lord, we know what we are, but know not
what we may be."—*Hamlet*, iv., 5.

IT is impossible to read Shakespeare with
the attention which his writings demand,
without very speedily coming to the conclusion that every word that is to be found in them
is there—not for the mere sake of contributing to
the euphony of a sentence, or giving a more musical
flow to the cadence of a line, but—with a good set

purpose:—and in like manner that every allusion, how vague soever it may appear to us with our imperfect knowledge of matters which were familiar as household words to Shakespeare and his contemporaries, has a clear and definite foundation, could we but trace it out.

A striking instance of this is shown in the few, apparently incoherent, words of Ophelia: " They say the owl was a baker's daughter." " This," says Warburton, " was a metamorphosis of the common people arising from the mealy appearance of the owl's feathers and her guarding the bread from mice." Steevens corrected this note of Warburton's, remarking, " To guard the bread from mice is rather the office of a cat than an owl"—and that " this was, however, no ' metamorphosis of the common people,' but a legendary story which both Dr. Johnson and myself have read, but in what book at least I cannot recollect."

And Steevens was right: for although the tale has not been discovered in any printed book, its existence as a common Gloucestershire story was ascertained by the late Mr. Douce; who relates it in one of the notes to the " Variorum Shakespeare" in the following words:—

" Our Saviour went into a baker's shop where they were baking, and asked for some bread to eat. The mistress of the shop immediately put a piece of dough into the oven to bake for him; but was reprimanded by her daughter, who, insisting that the piece of dough was too large, reduced it to a very small size. The dough, however, immediately afterwards began to swell, and presently became of a most enormous size. Whereupon the baker's daughter cried out,

' Heugh, heugh, heugh!'—which owl-like noise probably induced our Saviour for her wickedness to
transform her into that bird.   This story is often related to children to deter them from such illiberal
behaviour to poor people."

A writer in the " Gentleman's Magazine " for November, 1804 (pp. 1003-4), relates the following somewhat similar story, which he states to be well known
to the nurses in Herefordshire :—A certain fairy,
disguised as an old distressed woman, went into a
baker's shop and begged some dough of his daughter,
of whom she obtained a very small piece.   This she
further requested to bake in the oven; where it
swelling to the size of a large loaf, the baker's
daughter refused to let her have it.   She, however,
gave the pretended beggar another piece of dough,
but still smaller than the first.   This swelled in the
oven even more than the other; and was, in like
manner, retained.   A third and still smaller piece of
dough came out of the oven the largest of all, and
shared the same fate.   The disguised fairy, convinced
of the woman's covetousness by this repeated experiment, no longer restrained her indignation : she re-
sumed her proper form and struck the culprit with
her wand; who immediately flew out of the window
in the shape of an owl.

In Germany, as we learn from Grimm's " Deutsche
Mythologie,"* a legend of similar character is related
of the Cuckoo ; and it is to this wide-spread tradition
that allusion is made in the popular rhyme so current
throughout that country which is addressed to the

---

* S. 641.   Grimm quotes as his authority Prætorius Weltbeschreibung, I. 656, II. 491.

Cuckoo when he is heard for the first time, and in which he is invited to prognosticate what " length of days" the inquirer is destined to see:

Kukuk, Beckenknecht!	Cuckoo, Bakerwight!
Sag mir recht,	Tell me right,
Wie viel jahr Ich leben soll?	How many years I shall live?

and his meal-bedusted-looking feathers are referred to as affording proof of the truth of the legend. Whatever may be the origin of this remarkable legend— and that origin is at present involved in the greatest obscurity—the legend itself is very widely spread.

In Norway, the red-crested black Woodpecker is called Gertrudsbird; and in the Norwegian tales collected by Asbiornsen and Moe we find the following legend relating to it; which I translate,* because it furnishes at once a characteristic specimen of the popular stories of Norway, and a remarkable parallel to the tradition to which Shakespeare has alluded.

When our Saviour and St. Peter were wanderers upon the face of the earth, they came once upon a time to a woman who was standing at her kneading trough and kneading dough. Her name was Gertrud; and on her head she wore a red cap. As they had both journeyed over a great distance and were sore hungered, Our Saviour besought the woman to give them a morsel of bread. Yes, she said, they should have it; and she took a very small piece of dough and kneaded it; but it soon became so large, that it quite filled the kneading trough. No, that was a great deal too much—they could not have that.

---

* From the German translation of F. Breesemann, for I have never been able to procure the Danish original — entitled " Norske Folkeventyr."

Then she took a much smaller piece; but as she was kneading that, it became quite as large as the first piece. No, that was a great deal too much—they could not have that. The third time she took a very, very little piece; yet this time, also, it grew to be a great deal too much. "No, no, I can't give you anything," said Gertrud; "you must go your way without a meal, for the loaf always gets too big to give away." Then Our Lord was angered, and said, "Since thou hast a heart so wicked, and wilt not bestow upon me a morsel of bread, for a punishment thou shalt be transformed into a bird; and thou shalt seek thy food between the bark and the wood; and thou shalt never quench thy thirst but when the rain falleth!" And scarcely were the words spoken, before she was changed to a Gertruds-bird (Woodpecker), and flew away up the chimney; and even at the present day she is ofttimes seen flying about with her red cap upon her head and her whole body black—for the soot of the chimney had blackened her. And she is ever heard tapping and pecking the trees in search of food, and she always sings before rain—for she is for ever in want of drink.

III.

WAS SHAKESPEARE EVER A SOLDIER?

(1859.)

THE following Paper originally appeared in "Notes and Queries." The writer having sent one of the few separately printed copies to his kind and lamented friend the late Lord Lyndhurst, was told by that eminent judge of evidence, "that he had unquestionably proved his case." Another noble Lord (still happily among us), who has received the Thanks of Parliament for his ability and judgment displayed in support of great military operations, assured the writer that he had long felt convinced that Shakespeare must have served in the army, and that this belief had been strongly confirmed by witnessing the recent performance of his "Henry the Fifth." With such opinions in his favour, it will not be considered extraordinary if the writer considers that the question, Was Shakespeare ever a Soldier? must be resolved in the affirmative.

WAS SHAKESPEARE EVER A SOLDIER?

" Have I not heard great ordnance in the field?
.   .   .   .   .   .

Have I not in a pitched battle heard
Loud 'larums, neighing steeds, and trumpets clang?"
Taming of the Shrew.

IN the year 1843, when the expectancy of being relieved from a great portion of my official employments gave me a prospect of devoting my time more exclusively to literary pursuits, I sat down to a pleasing task which I had long prescribed to myself,—namely, that of making a minute examination into the writings of Shakespeare.

In this I had two especial objects; the one, and the only one to which I need now advert, being to ascertain how far such an examination made by another mind—that is, a mind differently constituted, although less gifted and far-sighted than those which had been already employed upon it—might discover in Shakespeare's writings the means of increasing the comparatively scanty materials which we possess for the biography of the poet.

Those labours were destined to be interrupted before I had accomplished one-half of my self-appointed task, but not until I had arrived at a conclusion, of the accuracy of which I now feel morally certain,— namely, that at some period of his life Shakespeare must have seen military service.

I arrived at this conclusion just about the time at which my friend Mr. Bruce discovered, or perhaps I should rather say was about to call attention to, the curious passage in a letter of Sir Philip Sidney, then engaged in the war of independence in the Low Countries, which forms the subject of the interesting paper entitled " Who was Will, my Lord of Leicester's jesting Player?" communicated by him to the first volume of the *Shakespeare Society's Papers;* and to which *Letter,* dated Utrecht, the 24th March, 1586, I shall have occasion hereafter to refer. I remember that the mutual communication of the point raised in that paper and my opinion took place in the same conversation—one was consequent upon the other; but whether I stated my opinion that Shakespeare had seen military service in consequence of Mr. Bruce's drawing my attention to Sidney's allusion to " Will, my Lord of Leicester's player," or he directed my attention to the passage in Sidney, on hearing my conviction that Shakespeare must have been a soldier, because I found his plays so horribly " stuff'd with epithets of war," I do not now recollect, nor is it material to the present inquiry.

The impression then made upon my mind has been deepened by subsequent consideration, and I trust before this paper is concluded that I shall convince my readers that Shakespeare has succeeded in describing all the " pride, pomp, and circumstance of glorious war " with such unrivalled skill, because, as Pope says,

" He best can paint them who has felt them most."

And here I may remind my readers that if Shakespeare served in the army, he is by no means the only poet of his age who did so. Aubrey tells us that Ben Jonson "went into the Lowe Countreys, and spent some time (not very long) in the armie, not to the disgrace of it, as you may find in his Epigrammes." "Gascoyne, Churchyard, Whetstone, Rich, and others" are enumerated by Mr. Collier ("Poetical Decameron," ii. 141) as among the phalanx of poets who united their endeavours under Elizabeth to free the Low Countries from the weight of the Spanish yoke: while the probability that Donne was engaged in military operations under Prince Maurice is shown not only by Marshall's portrait of him, but by the epigrams attributed to him, and which form the subject of Mr. Yeowell's communication to " N. & Q," 2nd S. iv. 49.

But, it may be asked, do the known facts of Shakespeare's life admit the possibility of his having ever encountered "the grappling vigour and rough frown of war?"

Let us see how far they are consistent with the supposition that he may have accompanied or followed the Earl of Leicester to the Low Countries. Leicester sailed from Harwich on the 4th, and landed at Flushing on the 10th December, 1585. He returned on 3rd December, 1586.

Now all that we know with certainty with respect to Shakespeare at this period is, that his twins, Hamnet and Judith, were born in February, 1585; and from that date until 1589, when we find him a sharer in the Blackfriars Theatre, nothing is really known as to where or how he was engaged.

It is clear, then, that it is quite possible that Shakespeare may have followed in Leicester's train. I think the passage in Sidney's Letter converts that possibility into something more than a probability. Let the reader judge for himself. The Letter, which is addressed to Secretary Walsyngham, Sidney's father-in-law, is dated "at Utrecht this 24th of March, 1586," and besides sentences which, as Mr. Bruce remarks, "seem to contain something like a foreshadowing of several of Shakespeare's noblest passages," contains the following allusion, as I believe, to Shakespeare:—

"I wrote to yow a Letter by *Will, my lord of Lester's jesting plaier*, enclosed in a letter to my wife, and I never had answer thereof. Hit contained something to my lord of Lester and council, that som wai might be taken to stay my ladi there. I since divers tymes have writt to know whether you had receaved them, but yow never answered me that point. I since find that *the knave* deliver'd the letters to my ladi of Lester, but whether she sent them yow or no I know not, but earnestly desire to do, because I dout there is more interpreted thereof."

After showing that there were four persons to whom Sidney may have referred, as Will, my Lord of Leicester's jesting player, namely, William Johnson, William Sly, William Kempe, (whom he believes to have been the "Will" alluded to), and William Shakespeare, Mr. Bruce expresses his conviction that Sir Philip Sidney never would have applied to Shakespeare the terms "jesting player" and "knave," even "allowing that the latter word might not be used in the modern offensive sense."

"Now that Shakespeare was a light-hearted, frolicsome man is clear from the deer-stealing; that he was witty in conversation is to be inferred from his daughter's epitaph; that he was termed 'Will Shakespeare' is certain; but I must at once express my own conviction that Sir Philip Sidney never could have applied to him the terms 'jesting player' and 'knave,' even allowing that the latter word might not be used in the modern offensive sense. Shakespeare's earliest works bear upon them the stamp of a mind far too contemplative and refined for its possessor ever to have been regarded as a jester or buffoon; besides which, the only traces that we have of him as an actor are in old Adam and the Ghost in Hamlet, certainly not humorous characters."

Mr. Bruce's opinion, that Shakespeare was not alluded to by Sidney is, it is obvious, mainly founded on his belief that Sidney could not and would not have designated Shakespeare as "knave" or "jesting." One word as to the epithet "knave." This, which our great dramatist himself makes Brutus apply to Lucius—

"Gentle knave, good night:"

and Anthony to Eros—

"My good knave, Eros"—

Sidney might without offence apply to Shakespeare, who was then, be it remembered, not the genius which the world now recognises, but the young fellow of two-and-twenty, a youth of promise indeed, but one whom Sidney perhaps knew best from his late deer-stealing peccadillo, as a roystering youngster with a nimble wit, a stout heart, and a ready hand.

But all who know my friend Mr. Bruce are aware of his great reverence, if I may so term it, for Shakespeare—a reverence which renders it almost impossible for him to conceive that Sidney, or indeed anybody, could apply to that mighty genius the epithets "knave" and "*jesting* player"—while, as he shares Johnson's "great contempt for that species of wit—puns," he is naturally disinclined to believe that Shakespeare's conversation was ever so marked or marred by the use of them as to earn for him the character of a "jesting" spirit.

I, on the other hand, have no doubt that of Shakespeare himself, whose whole mind was "quippish," it might almost be said, "not a word with him but a jest," and that his conversation, like his writings, was "full of odd quirks and remnants of wit;" and I feel sure that those who remember Johnson's remark, "that a quibble was to him the fatal Cleopatra for which he lost the world, and was content to lose it," will admit that I have some grounds for my belief. Besides, have we not Aubrey's report of his "very ready, pleasant, and smooth wit?" and does not Fuller, in his admirable account of his wit combats with Ben Jonson, speak especially of " the quickness of his wit and invention." I think, therefore, that at two-and-twenty he might deserve to be called " a jesting player."

I will now quote the passage in which Mr. Bruce then proceeds to show how great is the probability that the Earl of Leicester's players accompanied him into the Low Countries; and then, albeit unwilling to believe that Shakespeare could have been the "jesting player" and "knave" referred to by Sidney, he asks, " was not Shakespeare probably with them ?"

" He left Stratford after the birth of his twins, who were baptized in the month of February, 1585.

He is next traced as an important member of Lord Leycester's company of players, in 1589. He must have been in the company some considerable time, or he could not have attained the station which he held. Now the Earl was appointed to the command in the Low Countries in September, 1585, and immediately afterwards sent out letters to his friends and retainers, requesting them to accompany him thither. From Warwickshire, and especially from the neighbourhood of his domain at Kenilworth, his 500 men were in great part procured. One 'John Arden,' who was recommended to the earl's service by his relative and confidential servant Mr. Thomas Dudley,* and another, 'Thomas Ardern,' who was 'Clarcke Comptroller,'† were probably relatives of Shakespeare, and 'Miles Comes,' or, as he is afterwards termed, 'Miles Combes,'‡ was probably his neighbour. It was just about the time of the stir which this incident created in Warwickshire, that Shakespeare's father attained the lowest depth of his poverty, and that Shakespeare himself left his native town. The incidents may be altogether unconnected; but a young man of an excitable temperament, encumbered by an imprudent marriage and domestic difficulties—one to whom neither the world of Stratford nor its law was friendly—was of all persons the most likely to be affected by the general commotion around him. The departure of friends and neighbours would be to him

---

* Galba, c. viii. fo. 106.   † *Ibid.*, fo. 108.

‡ *Ibid.*, fo. 106. In the same MS. list of Leycester's servants, we find under the head of "Musiconer," the following names: "Thomas Cole, William Bainton, James Wharton, William Edgley, William Black, Jo, the harper, Walter, the boye." No players are mentioned.

a temptation and an example. They marshalled him the way that he should go; and although seeking distinction in other fields, stirred him up to find an arena for the exercise of that power which he must have felt within him. This consideration would lead to a conclusion very consonant with all we know of his biography; that he left home a little earlier than has been usually supposed. There may be nothing in it, but I point it out as a subject for investigation to those who feel an interest in such questions, and who have greater facilities for pursuing the necessary inquiries than I at present possess."

This was published in 1844, but by that time my leisure had passed away, and I could not accept the friendly challenge. It is only the circumstance of my having accidentally come across some of the notes which I then made on the subject of Shakespeare's "military acquirements," just after reading Lord Campbell's evidence of his "legal acquirements," that has induced me to undertake my present task of showing that, like George Gascoigne, who had also served in the Low Countries, Shakespeare might have adopted for his motto, " Tam Marti tam Mercurio."

But before I proceed to point out some of those passages in Shakespeare's writings which, as I contend, prove that at some time Shakespeare had seen

" The hand of Mars
Beckoning with fiery truncheon his retire,"

let me remind the reader that the fact of his having served under Leicester would go far to explain how he gained much of that familiarity with other things for which his writings are remarkable.

Thus, what he had observed when on shipboard, while on his way to the Low Countries and back (and let me point to a line in "Coriolanus" as an evidence of that observation—

> " As weeds before a vessel under sail,
> So men obey'd, and fell below his stem,")

may well have furnished him with that knowledge of seamanship discoverable in many of his plays, a knowledge which can only be acquired by those who go down to the sea in ships. His familiarity with the good points of a horse, and he is admitted to have described them with a skill which no other poet has ever attained to,—so that when he talks of horses, we see them

> " Printing their proud hoofs i' the receiving earth,"—

was probably acquired where " the army of the Queen had got the field." And we may here add, that if, as has been supposed from the allusions in his 37th and 89th Sonnets, he was lame—

> " Made lame by Fortune's dearest spite "—

the accident may well have happened to him while sharing in some of those encounters from witnessing which, as I believe, he acquired that knowledge of military matters of which his writings contain such abundant evidence.

One word more before I adduce the proofs that Shakespeare had seen military service derivable from his writings. The Lord Chief Justice, in investigating the evidence of Shakespeare's legal knowledge, had the advantage of being himself a master of the art on which he was treating, while I, in discussing Shakespeare's soldierly knowledge, have the disadvantage of being utterly incompetent to set a squadron in the field, and know no more than a spinster of the division of a battle.

Five-and-forty years had I lived in this happy land ere I had the necessity of taking in my hands a weapon of offence or defence; and when, on the memorable 10th of April, 1848, I was called upon to shoulder a brown bess, I know I did so with a strong feeling of apprehension, that, if unhappily compelled to use it, it might peradventure prove more dangerous to my Conservative friends than to the noisy Chartists against whom its fire would have been really directed.

My notes refer to Boswell's edition of *Malone*, the last *variorum* edition, which was published in 1821; and I will quote them in the order in which the plays are there inserted. I have no note of any soldierly allusions in "The Two Gentlemen of Verona," and I have only a memorandum of one such in

The Comedy of Errors,

Act iv. sc. 3., where Dromeo of Syracuse speaks of

" He that *sets up his rest* to do more exploits with his mace, than a morris pike."

And in reply to Antipholus' remark,

" What! thou meanest an officer?"

replies,

" Ay, Sir, the Serjeant of the Band. He that brings any man to answer, that breaks his band," &c.

Love's Labour's Lost.

In the first scene of the third act, between Armado and Moth, we have one slight reference:

" *Moth.* As swift as lead, Sir.
Arm. Thy meaning, pretty ingenious ?
Is not lead a metal heavy slow ?
Moth. Minimè, honest Master ; or rather, Master, no.
Arm. I say lead is slow.
Moth. . . . You are too swift, Sir, to say so :
Is that lead slow which is fired from a gun ?
Arm. . . . Sweet smoke of Rhetoricke,
He reputes me a cannon ; and the bullet, that's he :—
I shoot thee at the swain."

But in the same act, where Biron, speaking of

" This senior-junior, giant dwarf, Dan Cupid,"

exclaims,

" O my little heart !
And I to be a *Corporal of his field,*
And wear his colours like a tumbler's hoop !"

we have a direct professional allusion. Tyrwhitt
has shown, in a note on this passage from " Lord
Stafford's Letters," (vol. ii. p. 199) that a corporal of
the field corresponds to the aide-de-camp of the present day.

Passing by the "Merchant of Venice," the "Midsummer Night's Dream," and " The Taming of the
Shrew," as not containing any passages calling for
remark, I come to

ROMEO AND JULIET.

This play presents us with two or three similes
drawn from military experiences of a very striking
character. In act iii. sc. 3, when the nurse tells
how Juliet

" On Romeo cries
And then falls down again,"

Romeo's answer is of this character :

> " As if that name
> Shot from the deadly level of a gun
> Did murder her."

In the same scene we have another passage, the full force of which Steevens showed could only be understood by remembering that the English soldiers formerly used not even flint-locks but *match*-locks, and consequently were obliged to carry a *lighted match* hanging at their belts very near to the wooden flask in which they kept their powder,—an arrangement necessarily productive of many accidents. Shakespeare's recollection of some that he had witnessed probably led to his placing these words in the mouth of the Friar when reproving Romeo:

> " Thy wit, that ornament to shape and love,
> Mis-shapen in the conduct of them both,
> *Like powder in a skill-less soldier's flask,*
> Is set on fire by thine own ignorance,
> And thou dismembered with thine own defence."

I pass over the passage in scene 1, act v.,

> " And that the trunk may be discharged of breath
> As violently as hasty powder fir'd
> Doth hurry from the fatal cannon's womb,"

and come to the very striking image in the third scene, which was doubtless suggested to Shakespeare by his own recollections :

> " Thou art not conquer'd ; beauty's ensign yet
> Is crimson in thy lips, and in thy cheeks,
> And death's pale flag is not advanced there."

In the " Merry Wives of Windsor," we find him

placing a similar expression in the mouth of Fenton—

> "I must advance the colours of my love,
> And not retire."

As you Like it.

The only two passages in this play would not by themselves go far to support my views, but they may be noted as showing how readily Shakespeare drew his images from military subjects. The first is where Rosalind decides on assuming male attire :—

> "Were it not better,
> Because that I am more than common tall
> That I did suit me all points like a man ?
> A gallant curtle-ax upon my thigh,
> A boar spear in my hand, and (in my heart
> Lie there what hidden woman's fear there will)
> We'll have a swashing and a martial outside,
> As many other mannish cowards have,
> And do outface it with their semblances ;"

and the next (act. iii. sc. 4), where Celia, speaking of Orlando, says :—

> "O that's a brave man! he writes brave verses, speaks brave words, swears brave oaths, and breaks them bravely *quite traverse athwart* the heart of his lover; as a *puny tilter that spurs his horse but on one side breaks his staff*, like a noble goose."

Much Ado about Nothing.

Although Benedick gives a good picture of a soldier in his description of Claudio—

> "I have known when there was no musick with him *but the drum and fife*, and now had he rather hear the tabor and pipe; I have known when he would have walked ten miles a-foot to see a *good armour ;* and now will he lie ten nights awake carving the fashion of a new doublet. He was wont to speak plain and to the purpose, like an honest man and a soldier; and now is he turned orthographer."—Act ii. sc. 3.

Yet the military allusions in this admirable Comedy are but few. Some of these, however, are so purely technical that they have been left unexplained by the commentators.

Thus Benedick asks Claudio how he will wear his willow garland—

"About your neck like an usurer's chain, or under your arm *like a lieutenant's scarf*."—Act ii. sc. 1.

Again, in the fifth act, sc. 2, where Benedick tells Margaret "I give thee the Bucklers," we have abundance of illustrations to tell us that the phrase is equivalent to "I yield," but we have never a word to illustrate his meaning when he says,

"You must put in the pikes with a vice,"

a phrase clearly borrowed by Shakespeare from the language of the camp, and which, though obviously technical, I confess myself quite as unable to explain as my predecessors.*

---

* I am indebted to the kindness of my accomplished friend Mr. Albert Way for the following able explanation. The circular "bucklers" of the sixteenth century, now called more commonly targets, had frequently a central spike, or "pike" usually affixed by a screw. It was probably found convenient to detach this spike occasionally; for instance, in cleaning the buckler, or in case of that piece of defensive armor being carried about on any occasion when not actually in use. A sharp projecting spike, four or five inches long, would obviously be inconvenient. As an example of the fashion of making it moveable and formed with a screw to affix it to the buckler, it will suffice to refer to the target of the Emperor Charles V. in the Armory at Goodrich Court, figured in Skelton's Illustrations of that Collection, vol. i. pl. 53. The date of this target is about 1550. In Skelton's plate the spike with its screw is represented full size; it measures in length, the screw included,

HAMLET.

In this magnificent specimen of Shakespeare's genius, we have, as I think, many traces of his brief military career. His description of a Ghost,

> "Armed at point exactly cap-à-pie,"

may not be one of these ; but when he speaks of his " wearing his bever *up*," it is clear from Bullokar that he was correct in so describing the helmet— for "bever" was in his time used to signify that part of the helmet which when *up* exposed the face of the wearer, although, as Malone tells us, it properly signified that which was let *down* to enable the wearer to drink.

When Fortinbras, at the close, directs that Hamlet shall be buried with the same honours that he would have received had he been slain in battle—

> "And for his passage,
> The soldier's musick and the rites of war
> Speak loudly for him,"

5¼ inches. "Vice" is the French *vis*, a screw, a word still in common use, the female screw being called *écrou*. Cotgrave gives " *vis*, the vice or spindle of a presse ;" namely, a strong wooden screw, such as we see in a cheese-press, a press for cider, and the like. Palsgrave gives only " Vyce of a cuppe, *vis ;*" namely, a screw in the bottom or stem, fixing its various parts or ornaments together. From resemblance to a screw a winding or turret staircase was called a Vice, as in the Promptorium Parvulorum,—" Vyce, rownde grece or steyer, *coclea*." The term is not uncommon in the Wicliffite Version, in old building contracts, &c.; for instance, that for building Fotheringay church, 1435. It may suffice to cite Chaucer's Dream, v. 1312, where he relates how, suddenly awaking in the stillness of the night,—

> "I rise and wallet sought pace and pace,
> Till I a winding staire found ;
> And held the vice aye in my hond,
> And upward softly so gan creepe."

K

we have probably a reminiscence of funeral honours which Shakespeare himself had witnessed.   But can it be doubted that when he says:

> " And let it work :
> For 'tis the sport *to have the engineer*
> *Hoist with his own petard.*"—Act iii. sc. 4.

or when he speaks of Slander:

> " Whose whisper o'er the world's diameter,
> *As level as the cannon to his blank,*
> Transports his poisoned shot."—Act iv. sc 2.

that we have images drawn from his own military experiences ?

Are the following less striking proofs of this ?

> " O my dear Gertrude, this
> Like to a *murdering piece,* in many places
> Give me superfluous death."

The "murdering piece" being in Shakespeare's time a specific term for a piece of ordnance, or small cannon, charged with small bullets, nails, &c., and well calculated therefore to "give superfluous death."

How entirely technical is the allusion in Hamlet's letter to Horatio:

> " I have words to speak in thine ear shall make thee dumb ; yet are they *much too light for the bore* of the matter."

Nor is the following allusion to the proving of cannon one jot less so:

> " Therefore this project
> Should have a back, or second, that might hold
> If this should *blast in proof.*"—Act iv. sc. 7.

A few lines previously the King speaks of Laertes choosing

> " A sword *unbated;* and in a *pass of practice*
> Requite him for your father"—

terms obviously drawn from military experience. Let us hope that the following was not drawn from Shakespeare's own:

> " Methought I lay
> Worse than the *mutines in the bilboes.*"

MERRY WIVES OF WINDSOR.

The military allusions in this play are few, but characteristic.   Bardolph speaks of " conclusions passed *the carieres*," and Ford, act iii. sc. 2, tells us—

" Why this boy will carry a letter twenty miles *as easy as a cannon will shoot point blank* twelve score."

The most striking, however, is where Falstaff describes himself when packed in the buck-basket as being—

" Compassed, like a good bilbo, in the circumference of a peck, hilt to point, heel to head."—Act iii. sc. 5.

For the simile is drawn from the flexibility of the Spanish blades made at Bilboa, and which were renowned for their excellence in the field.

TROILUS AND CRESSIDA.

An attentive perusal of this play alone would, I think, convince any unprejudiced reader that, at some period of his life, Shakespeare must have witnessed the operations of war, so full is it of epithets, similes, and allusions drawn from such a source.   While any one who admits the possibility of Shakespeare having accompanied Leicester to the Low Countries will probably share my belief that in pourtraying the contests between the Greek and Trojan hosts, he but recorded his recollections of encounters between the forces of England and the United Provinces and those under the Duke of Alva.

We have the very " Prologue " armed, and telling us that " our play leaps o'er the vaunt."

The " *hacks* on Hector's helmet," " the *ward* at which Cressid was won't to lie," are but small matters compared to the picture drawn by Ulysses of the distraction in the Grecian camp, and which resemble those which Shakespeare might himself have witnessed in the camp of the allies—

> " The General's disdained
> By him one step below ; he, by the next ;
> The next by him beneath."

Who can doubt when Patroclus plays old Nestor,—

> " And with a palsy-fumbling on his gorget,
> Shakes in and out the rivet "—

that Shakespeare drew the picture from the life ; or that he had any other source for the following :—

> " So that *the ram, that batters down the wall,*
> For the great swing and rudeness of his poize,
> They place before the hand that made the engine ;
> Or those that with the fineness of their souls,
> By reason guide his execution."—Act i. sc. 3.

Nestor's message—

> " I'll hide my silver beard in a gold *beaver*,
> And in my *vantbrace* put this withered brawn."

Agamemnon's comparison of Achilles—

> " *Like an engine*
> *Not portable*"—

Cassandra speaking of " *notes of sally*"—Troilus' allusion to the—

> " Hand of Mars
> Beckoning with *fiery truncheon* my retire"—

Hector's—

> " I like thy armour well,
> I'll *frush* it, and *unlock the rivets all*"—

and the allusions to the wearing of "gloves" and "sleeves"—the threat,

> " For I will *throw my glove* to death himself,"—

the picture,

> " Or like a gallant horse fall'n in first rank,
> Lie there for pavement to the abject rear
> O'errun and trampled on,"—

and the reference to the "sticklers" who separate the armies,—are all redolent of the camp, and could I think scarcely have been learned in any other school.

I pass by

MEASURE FOR MEASURE,

in which the allusions of this character are but scant, that I may come to

OTHELLO,

which abounds with them.   The space which I have already occupied is, however, so very large, that I must condense the passages as much as possible. The well-known description of Cassio—

> "That never set a squadron in the field,
> Nor the division of a battle knows
> More than a spinster,"—

the distinction between "lieutenant" and "ancient" —the allusion to

> "The curse of service,
> Preferment goes by letter and affection,
> Not by the old gradation,"—

are among many instances.

And—

" When he's old *cashiered*,"—

" I must show out a sign and *flag of love*,"—

" For that it stands not in *such warlike brace*,"—

" Men do their broken weapons rather use
Than their bare hands,"—

"The tyrant custom, most brave senators,
Hath made the flinty and steel couch of war
My thrice driven bed of down,"—

" Let housewives make a skillet of my helm,"—

" *Cas.* What an eye she hath—methinks it sounds a *parley*
of provocation.

Iago. And when she speaks, is it not *an alarm* to love ?"—

" And stood within *the blank* of his displeasure,"—

" Whose solid virtue
The *shot* of accident, nor dart of chance
Could neither graze, nor pierce,"—

" It is a sword of Spain, the icebrook's temper
.   .   .   .
A better never did sustain itself
Upon a soldier's thigh,"—

show how much of Shakespeare's imagery was drawn
from the " tented field."

Who can doubt that from that " tented field," and
the stern necessities of discipline he had there witnessed, he learned that

" Wars must make examples
Out of the best"—

and only repeated what he had himself heard from
some officer, suppressing a broil in the camp, when
he makes Othello exclaim

" What! in a town of war
Yet wild, the people's hearts brimful of fear,
To manage private and domestic quarrel,
In night, and on the court of guard and safety !
'Tis monstrous."

Who can doubt that it was under the inspiration of having shared in the dangers and excitement of a campaign, that Shakespeare put into the mouth of the noble Moor his chivalrous and touching farewell to military glory :—

> "Farewell the plumed troop and the big wars
> That make ambition virtue! O farewell!·
> Farewell the neighing steed and the shrill trump,
> The spirit-stirring drum, the ear-piercing fife,
> The royal banner ; and all quality,
> Pride, pomp, and circumstance of glorious war!
> And O you mortal engines, whose rude throats
> The immortal Jove's dread clamours counterfeit,
> Farewell! Othello's occupation's gone!"

Those only know the full pathos of these words who have heard them uttered by Edmund Kean.

Fortunately for my readers—unluckily, perhaps, for my own theory—here my Notes came to an end. I was interrupted by graver duties before I had time to examine the Historical Plays; otherwise I have no doubt I should have found in them confirmation, "strong, as holy writ," of the views which I entertain.

But incomplete as was my examination of Shakespeare's dramatic writings, I had from such examination gathered enough to convince me that, in discoursing of military matters, Shakespeare was no "bookish theorick;" that "mere prattle, without practice," was not "all his soldiership." I felt this, and felt assured that time would prove it so.

That time to my mind came when Mrs. Green published, in August, 1857, her *Calendar of State Papers, Domestic Series of the Reign of James I.,* 1603—1610, and in it a notice of " The names of the trained soldiers within the hundred of Barlich-

way, taken at Alcester the 23rd September, 1605,"
the year of the Gunpowder Plot, before Sir Fulke
Greville and Sir Edward Greville, and Thomas
Spencer, Esq., under the command of Capt. Hayles,
in which, under the head of Rowington, occurs the
name of " WILLIAM SHAKESPEARE."*

" Shakespeares," says Mr. Collier, " were unquestionably numerous in Warwickshire, and in some
of the adjoining counties; but we have intelligence
regarding no other William Shakespeare at that date,
in that part of the kingdom." And when it is remembered, not only that Barlichway is the hundred
in which Stratford-upon-Avon is situated, but that
Rowington figures prominently in the Shakespeare
pedigree,—that, as appears from his will, the poet at
the time of his death held one copyhold tenement
with appurtenances, lying and being in Stratford-
upon-Avon in the county of Warwick, " being par-
cel or holden of the mannour of Rowington," I
think few of my readers will deny that I have succeeded in my endeavour to establish the fact that
SHAKESPEARE WAS A SOLDIER.

* " Athenæum (No. 1555), August 15th, 1857; " Collier's
Shakespeare " (ed. 1858), vol. i., p. 181.

CHISWICK PRESS:—PRINTED BY WHITTINGHAM AND WILKINS,
TOOKS COURT, CHANCERY LANE.

CPSIA information can be obtained at www.ICGtesting.com
Printed in the USA
BVOW03s2320040214

344002BV00009B/125/P